Anthony is a middle-aged first-generation Australian, whose passion for words and expression began during his later years of high school during the last millennia. Although detoured by life, he has since found his way back to his passion.

When not writing, you can find Anthony exploring his other passions and hobbies, whether relating to technology, enjoying the solitude nature provides, observing the natural world or photographing severe weather events and phenomena.

I have been blessed to have known three remarkable women, whom share similar qualities of strength, independence, intelligence, warmth, compassion, empathy and love and yet, each uniquely their own person.

Our paths crossed serendipitously along this journey, a journey we refer to as life. However, I feel as serendipitous as it may appear; there is always a reason; a greater plan to why souls connect.

Two have since passed away and they will always hold a place in my heart.

Then there is one. She saw through the man hiding in plain sight, she saw through me and patiently waited. She fanned the smouldering ember within, to set the fire ablaze. She not only unlocked my emotions I'd suppressed, she won my heart when I thought I would never love or be loved again.

I know these are but words upon a piece of paper, but they are words arising from the depths of my heart.

Anthony Superina

BEHIND BLUE EYES

AUSTIN MACAULEY PUBLISHERS™
LONDON • CAMBRIDGE • NEW YORK • SHARJAH

Copyright © Anthony Superina 2024

The right of Anthony Superina to be identified as author of this work has been asserted by the author in accordance with sections 77 and 78 of the Copyright, Designs and Patents Act 1988.

All rights reserved. No part of this publication may be reproduced, stored in a retrieval system, or transmitted in any form or by any means, electronic, mechanical, photocopying, recording, or otherwise, without the prior permission of the publishers.

Any person who commits any unauthorised act in relation to this publication may be liable to criminal prosecution and civil claims for damages.

All of the events in this memoir are true to the best of the author's memory. The views expressed in this memoir are solely those of the author.

A CIP catalogue record for this title is available from the British Library.

ISBN 9781035822386 (Paperback)
ISBN 9781035822393 (ePub e-book)

www.austinmacauley.com

First Published 2024
Austin Macauley Publishers Ltd®
1 Canada Square
Canary Wharf
London
E14 5AA

Introduction

Well, hello there!

I like to believe I'm creative, even imaginative. Never would I have envisioned this present if you asked me five, ten or twenty years ago. I doubt the most talented scriptwriters or novelists of the past and present could have conceived such an epic.

There are days where I close my eyes, fall asleep and hope when I awaken come the morning, this has been a nightmare. Here we are now and without doubt, this is my reality…living life as a young widower.

I must not forget…every nightmare has a twist, and this is no different.

Although it might not appear in the manner, the journey you're about to embark is from various journal entries and my memories. In addition, what I'm about to reveal is of periods in my life. Some locations and names have been altered in order to honour and protect those now passed and those still living.

Life can be much stranger than fiction.

Chapter 1

I could begin simply by taking you back to the late 1990s. Some may remember the era from just the mere mention of the nineties. Where would the fun be if we didn't at least revisit that moment in time? Oh, that's right! Those memories would still be memories, meandering my endless mind.

So, get ready, as we need to delve back a couple of decades, a century and, not forgetting, a millennium to where the journey began.

It was the latter half of the 90s. The world had since witnessed the first Gulf War, the Beatles Anthology, the birth of Windows 95, the beginning of the Internet age and more. I was in my second year of full-time employment and the world was readying for the looming millennium and panicking over the millennium bug, better known as Y2K. The sensationalism of the press and the pockets of hysteria still makes me laugh. The Internet on a community scale was still relatively new and small by comparison to today's staggering user count! Dial-up modems were common…who could forget that infamous collage of sound as systems were connecting, the lightning 56kbps speed and the risk you would take each time you connected, hoping that no one

Anthony Superina

BEHIND BLUE EYES

AUSTIN MACAULEY PUBLISHERS™
LONDON • CAMBRIDGE • NEW YORK • SHARJAH

Copyright © Anthony Superina 2024

The right of Anthony Superina to be identified as author of this work has been asserted by the author in accordance with sections 77 and 78 of the Copyright, Designs and Patents Act 1988.

All rights reserved. No part of this publication may be reproduced, stored in a retrieval system, or transmitted in any form or by any means, electronic, mechanical, photocopying, recording, or otherwise, without the prior permission of the publishers.

Any person who commits any unauthorised act in relation to this publication may be liable to criminal prosecution and civil claims for damages.

All of the events in this memoir are true to the best of the author's memory. The views expressed in this memoir are solely those of the author.

A CIP catalogue record for this title is available from the British Library.

ISBN 9781035822386 (Paperback)
ISBN 9781035822393 (ePub e-book)

www.austinmacauley.com

First Published 2024
Austin Macauley Publishers Ltd®
1 Canada Square
Canary Wharf
London
E14 5AA

I would like to graciously extend my heartfelt thanks to my publisher, Austin Macauley, and all the team members who worked diligently behind the scenes. Their efforts have provided me with an amazing opportunity and brought my idea to life, turning it into a reality. I am truly grateful for their support and dedication.

I must also acknowledge someone very special to me, my late wife Dee. Without her unwavering support and belief in me, this moment would not have been possible. Even during the times I came to doubt myself, she never wavered her faith in my abilities. She always believed in the potential of my words and the impact they could have on others. Forever am I grateful for her encouragement and love.

Introduction

Well, hello there!

I like to believe I'm creative, even imaginative. Never would I have envisioned this present if you asked me five, ten or twenty years ago. I doubt the most talented scriptwriters or novelists of the past and present could have conceived such an epic.

There are days where I close my eyes, fall asleep and hope when I awaken come the morning, this has been a nightmare. Here we are now and without doubt, this is my reality…living life as a young widower.

I must not forget…every nightmare has a twist, and this is no different.

Although it might not appear in the manner, the journey you're about to embark is from various journal entries and my memories. In addition, what I'm about to reveal is of periods in my life. Some locations and names have been altered in order to honour and protect those now passed and those still living.

Life can be much stranger than fiction.

Chapter 1

I could begin simply by taking you back to the late 1990s. Some may remember the era from just the mere mention of the nineties. Where would the fun be if we didn't at least revisit that moment in time? Oh, that's right! Those memories would still be memories, meandering my endless mind.

So, get ready, as we need to delve back a couple of decades, a century and, not forgetting, a millennium to where the journey began.

It was the latter half of the 90s. The world had since witnessed the first Gulf War, the Beatles Anthology, the birth of Windows 95, the beginning of the Internet age and more. I was in my second year of full-time employment and the world was readying for the looming millennium and panicking over the millennium bug, better known as Y2K. The sensationalism of the press and the pockets of hysteria still makes me laugh. The Internet on a community scale was still relatively new and small by comparison to today's staggering user count! Dial-up modems were common...who could forget that infamous collage of sound as systems were connecting, the lightning 56kbps speed and the risk you would take each time you connected, hoping that no one picked up the receiver or someone tried to call, especially if you weren't fortunate to have call-waiting!

Some people even had an additional line installed with a private number dedicated to the Internet. Children from at least the mid-naughties and on will never know the challenges and stresses involved in connecting to the World Wide Web!

It was certainly a different time, as is each decade before and after. Yes, you had your malware and predators and your Nigerian email scams, but it was a time where people from around the world could connect without the need of paying thousands of dollars to travel abroad for a couple of weeks. There were a variety of methods to connect. There was AOL Messenger, MSN Messenger, Mirabilis ICQ and Tribal Voice's PowWow to name but a few of the more popular programs of the time. Honestly, these were fantastic programs that allowed instant messaging, file transfers, voice recordings, video calls (albeit in its infancy) and group chats. Decades later, we as a society take these features for granted.

I was an early adopter of ICQ, establishing friendships from around the world and from around the country, too. I cannot remember who it was, but one of those friends suggested I should try this relatively new program called PowWow. Being curious, how was I able to resist? Of course, me being me, I wasn't about to jump in blindly, so I did my due diligence and researched what was available, which was quite limited if you were to compare to today's Internet! Anyhow, with the information at hand, I just said to myself, "Why not…what do I have to lose!" and I started the lengthy and agonising download. Geez…to download a five-megabyte file could take anywhere between a few minutes (if lucky) to a point where you had time to make yourself a meal, eat the meal, relax for a bit, have a shower and return to still find that you had a handful of minutes remaining! There were even instances where the connection with the server would freeze, leaving the calculated time remaining in the years! I would love to say I am embellishing my memory, but I cannot.

Having installed and configured PowWow, I found it quite easy to navigate and use, particularly of the similarities to that of ICQ. The one feature that caught my attention was that of community rooms, a feature lacking from ICQ. A few dozen rooms existed besides many private rooms. If memory serves me well, when trying to find a room from a list, you just had a name of the room, the number of people, and if the room was moderated or private. I remember scrolling through the list of rooms, trying to determine which one I should enter. By fortune or a little serendipitous intervention, I haplessly stumbled my way into the Dew Drop Inn. Try saying that ten times over in rapid succession when tired!

Before I continue any further, it is necessary to reveal a back story for context and it will definitely support in building the foundation to continue along this journey.

I was a young adult at the time and, as I was discovering who I was and trying to navigate the world, I felt the world was conspiring against me. Nothing truly prepares you for the reality of everyday life, the ups and the downs you will encounter and being of a young age, it can become overwhelming quickly. For myself, I have always pondered things like…why does humanity exist…what happens after death…what my purpose is…I still ponder these and the millions of other thoughts meandering in my mind. Anyhow, through these eyes, I felt my life was spiralling; I was losing control and that I may not correct the spiral. I had no one to turn to, and for those very few who know me will understand that remark. Not only was it a difficult time, as I reflect, I realise I was lonely. I enjoy being alone, but there is a difference between that of loneliness and that of being alone. The feelings of the time would be dwarfed by what the future had waiting for me.

If I knew what I do today, I still believe I would take the same paths at each fork along this journey. Maybe I'm a sucker who enjoys challenges!

So, now with that back story out of the way, we can get this journey moving once again!

Upon entering the Dew Drop Inn, I was immediately greeted, no wait…I was interrogated. I was asked a range of questions, a sign of profiling. Nothing like entering a room and being interrogated. Instinctively or foolishly, depending on how you wish to interpret it, I mashed the keys on my keyboard to answer some of their questions. I am not one you can intimidate. I will, however, make a quick calculation of the situation and act accordingly. As soon as I hit enter and my response went live to the world, the barrage of verbal abuse begun! I can only imagine what you must think, "The Internet doesn't seem any different to what it is today." Well, yes, and no. Yes, people abused, attacked and bullied using the guise of anonymity; such occurrences were rare. Coming from a sporting background, the barrage was quite amusing! For one, the sledging was mediocre, their spelling needed quite some work and if I was to redact the profanity, there wouldn't be more than a few words, thus making no sense.

This would continue for at least five minutes, I estimate…I wasn't timing it, but it seemed to drag on. The barrage came to an abrupt end when the next unsuspecting visitor entered. With the lynch mob's attention now diverted, I decided I would stick around. Come on, how could I just up and leave after such a profound welcoming! It would be rude of me. Now, I could quietly observe! In time, my observations would reveal most of the lynch mob being men with two women contributing. These people in one form of another were in a relationship, whether friends, extended family or immediate family. There was definitely a relationship connection coming through. They were attempting to make the Dew Drop Inn their own chatroom, although they could have established a private room.

By doing so, they would lose access to the public and unsuspecting victims—play toys. People just wanted to see if they could connect with people from around the world and possibly their own country. What astounded me with the actions of a minority, their chats remained publicly visible. They could have created a group chat by invite only. During a lull in visitors, they would freely and arrogantly boast of their private lives. All the men came from a particular branch of the US military.

Having enough information and enough of the bullshit, I could no longer quietly remain in the proverbial shadows, observing. The chat or maybe I should refer to it as a confrontation, I remember vividly. I will not go into detail, but allow me to just say they did not appreciate the references and history fed to them. They attempted to respond, emphasising their belief in their superiority and continually repeating it. It was at this moment, other people in the community saw an opportunity. There was a seismic shift of spirit, leading to an unprecedented barrage of words upon the ignorant. Two responses changed and featured more of a threatening undertone, but I wasn't all too concerned.

After the chaos and the dust settling, the lynch mob departed. I considered departing, but I stuck around longer. Newcomers entering no longer faced the ugly side of a minority. They could feel at ease and safe; introducing themselves to whoever, engaging in conversations that could lead to the discovery of new connections, friendships and possibly more! That was the theory behind the community chatroom; to bring people together.

As the room settled, the environment was quite enjoyable, but the time had passed me by. I was considering logging off for the evening and definitely, I would return. Before I could exit, I received a message from a user who thanked me for standing up and asked if they could add me to their friend's list. Of course, being me, I felt uncomfortable accepting any thanks, and I accepted their friend request. And that is where this journey ends. Nah, just kidding! Having accepted the request from a Dee, shortly after, Dee sent an instant message, depicted by the sound of a barking dog. Once more, Dee thanked me and told me not to worry about any of the threats. She would also formally introduce herself. I replied, formally introducing myself, and told her I had already forgotten about any threats. I mentioned how it was lovely to have met her, and I hoped I would chat with her some more, for I was logging off for the evening.

In retrospect, this message would change the course of my life, or at least where I thought my life was heading. Who could have conceived such a message would possess such an impact!

The next day would begin with us re-connecting and chatting. This would soon become an everyday occurrence, first through PowWow and then later through ICQ.

There was no small talk; our conversations were deep and meaningful, compassionate, amusing and silly. We could easily jump from topic to topic without missing a beat. It was wonderful to talk with someone on the same wavelength. As I reminisce, I'm taken back to each moment and the sound bytes we shared. Amazingly, I still have the files and maybe one day, I will don the headphones, listen and indulge in those memories. You never know what the future holds and there are some things worth holding on to. Anyway, over the coming months, we would split time between PowWow and ICQ, sometimes interacting on both platforms at the same time; just for a bit of amusement with the sounds of barking dogs and uh-ohs alternating. As the days rolled into weeks and the weeks morphed into months, we incorporated the telephone into our conversations. Those conversations were amazing, and also challenging. To hear her voice, the tonality and the other titbits provided another level of insight into the woman. The challenge was that of time zones and costs, but we put our heads together to arrive at a solution; you might say we found middle ground. Dee would do most of the calling, for she had easy access to pre-paid international calling cards with amazing rates. Here, it was challenging to find international calling cards, but the genuine challenge was finding a card with comparable rates. The cards weren't all that much cheaper than the rates attached to a standard home phone plan. While she took on most of the cost, I would make sure I was available to talk during the early hours of the morning, which made it early to late afternoon State side. We did chat at other times and I also made calls.

Communication, time, respect and compromise are keys to any relationship, friendship or partnership. Take either from the equation and the foundation becomes unsteady.

Dee would purchase a fifty-dollar card. That card would last anywhere between seven to twenty-one days, depending on the number of calls made, the time of day, and the length of the call. On average, we spoke once a day for at least three to four hours. There was a weekend in there where we spoke twice on a Saturday (Friday and Saturday for her) for eight hours. When you are comfortable, it is just natural to be in the presence of that person. While on costs, I had a sharp learning curve! My phone bill at the time was quarterly and very affordable. Having made a few calls to Dee at length only highlighted the phrase 'out of sight, out of mind'. Well, when you receive a bill in-excess of three thousand dollars, you're shocked! Once you compose yourself, allowing the shock to pass, you then test out your profanity vocabulary before settling into a state of relative calmness.

Although it was shocking, in the end it didn't matter. It was merely money that I could recoup with time. However, the time I could spend with Dee was not only quality, but priceless.

If you truly care and love someone, you don't pass up an opportunity to spend time with them. Today, we have video calls to connect, something that wasn't available. The opportunities you miss are opportunities lost! And let's not forget, today could be our last day, or that day could be in eighty years. We just don't know, so don't waste precious time.

Anyway, it was around a year to a year and a half into our friendship that I realised I had developed intense feelings for Dee. These feelings were an accumulation of many factors, not just the physical that seems so highly emphasised today. Taking this journey and reflection, I am thankful that we had time apart. We built a friendship, and yet, it provided the time to allow us to discover one another's personality, character, heart and soul.

This is but my opinion, but the person you love is your best friend, albeit your intimate best friend. You will spend most of your time with them, you will want to make and share memories of experiences, and they are the one who'll share in the good and the bad times. They are the one who you come home to.

Physical beauty will fade over time, but the beauty possessed within will remain.

Distance is merely temporary and can be time-consuming. As I have since discovered, as you become older and wiser, that distance is agony. Maybe it's because of my experiences or that you come to realise how amazing it is to have someone in your life and life is fleeting.

The distance provided us with the time to explore our feelings. I would also learn, albeit some years later, before I would realise, two discoveries of enlightenment. The first being distance means so little when someone means so much, and with a little patience, opportunities arise. It isn't easy to be patient when you want to be in the same room. The second being of respect, trust, communication and love from afar. When entering a long distance relationship, you need to prioritise time with each other, communicate, no matter how difficult the topic; set aside egos and share in each other's daily lives, no matter how insignificant you may find it.

Let's get back on the journey after that important digression. Having realised I was falling in love, I didn't react. It was a combination of being scared and not really knowing how to react. It scared me that if I was to tell Dee of my feelings, the friendship would crumble. And for not knowing how to react…well, was I definitively sure of my love or was it more lust? So, I decided not to say anything; seeing how those feelings progressed over the next few weeks. Of course, those feelings didn't fade. I would say they intensified. I was sure that I was in love with her. Some of you may roll your eyes, arguing and questioning. We as a society might attempt to define the structure of falling in love, but I believe love finds you during your weakest moment, for anyone can love another at their best. Only true hearts and genuine love can endure when we are at our lowest. Life is of patterns, as life is always in flow. Having worked up the courage, my plan was to reveal my love for her during our next phone call. Okay, maybe not the next phone call, but at least the call on the upcoming Sunday. Well, Sunday arrived a tad faster than I expected, or I lost an entire day!

It was a late Saturday afternoon; the phone unexpectedly rang. I say unexpectedly, as my number was a private one, and a part from the Telco, Dee was the only person to have it. Of course, someone could have dialled a wrong number or a telemarketing company, but that wasn't all that likely. It was Dee, and we just fell into one of our usual conversations, where time stood still. She had an early start the following day and still had a few errands to run. She quickly mentioned that we'll chat again soon and in the softest of voices, she uttered the words, "I love you" and quickly hung up. I was taken aback! It took a moment for what happened to register. I was a little disappointed that she beat me to the punch, but I now knew how she felt. I could only imagine what she must have endured, knowing those three words could not be unheard and not knowing of the other person's feelings.

Another twenty-four hours would pass before our next call. The call again started like every other call, but this time during a moment of opportunity, I mentioned I thought I heard her say something at the end of the call. Being coy, I mentioned I wasn't sure what she said, but I thought it sounded like I love you? There was a moment of an eerie silence; Dee's voice breaking through, telling me I heard correctly, but she hoped it was quiet enough that I didn't hear. She wasn't sure how I would react. Immediately, I opened up and explained how she beat me to the punch, as I had planned to tell her that day. Let's just say we enjoyed a good laugh, which helped ease the anxiety as well as creating a lasting memory.

How wonderful is the clarity of hindsight! It would be useful if it was present sight! Emotions are hard to decipher at the best of times, but add heightened emotions into the mix. You don't want to feel like the fool dealing with the emotions associated with rejection and heartache. With our relationship progressing, we began speaking more about the future, and our future in particular. As I reflect, the importance of 'our future' was becoming the main-stay of our conversations. We came to the arrangement that Dee would fly out to Australia. It just seemed the wiser and logical option of the time. Although I was ready to fly to be with her, there was a period where every attempt she made to leave was thwarted in the eleventh hour. It was becoming frustrating for both of us and years later when we spoke of the events, we both had thoughts that maybe it wasn't meant to be, but neither one of us acted on our thoughts and we continued to fight for what we had and what we could have. To say it wasn't difficult would be a lie! The body and heart had craved her, the missing piece, so to speak. Our paths crossed for a reason and I didn't just want a friend; I wanted a lover, a confidant, a best friend, a muse and someone I could create and share a lifetime of memories while taking on life together.

If memory serves me correctly, Dee made at least three attempts to fly out, each time thwarted. Anyway, I had enough and I would take matters into my own hands. It was a Saturday morning; I called a travel agent and booked a flight to the United States. I remember telling my mum that I just bought a ticket. She was quite supportive, telling me if I truly had feelings for her, find out, otherwise you'll be left either regretting or wondering. Come Monday, arriving at work, no one had a clue what was to come. I was the reliable, quiet worker, working my way from crushing boxes for recycling to shipping and receiving and the go-to IT guy for in-house issues. Just before clocking off, I walked up to my manager, who wasn't the most personable of persons, and asked for a word in private. I informed him I was officially handing in my notice. The look on his face was priceless! Upon composing himself, he asked if I was sure before beginning the process. I was sure and in the future, I would be sure once again when faced with a similar decision, despite ignoring my intuition.

Taking a moment...I am sure many of you, having just finished reading to this point, must think I lost my sanity! Who in the right mind buys a ticket to travel halfway across the world and quits their job for love? Let's add to the equation that we had yet to physically meet, so there was no idea of the sexual compatibility or chemistry. She could've been a serial killer! If she was, I would have my fifteen minutes of fame and become a part of history.

Well, I did and I would likely do it again!

I will admit, it is highly irregular for me or someone with a similar personality to rush or act spontaneously. It doesn't imply it never happens; when it does, it is more impactful and memorable. Rushing into love can expose you to a potential world of heartache and pain. Nevertheless, we know not of the time we have left and we have but one life to live, so when I love, it is all of me or none of me. Having mentioned how I love reminded me how years later; Dee would describe it from her perspective. She emphasised loyalty, empathy, compassion, intimacy, romance, passion, support, adoration, patient, understanding, listener, space, championing, growth, protector, headaches and unconditional love. She mentioned that it's a unique experience to have someone love you more than they love themselves.

Just recalling those words has saltwater welling in my eyes.

My last day of work was less than a week before my departure. I am not one for the spotlight, and yet I couldn't avoid it. Two co-workers attempted to track me down, no matter how well I tried to avoid them. They had the upperhand by working together. They only learnt of my departure that morning and were quite shocked to see me leave. Because of the relationship I had with them, I filled them in on my reasoning. Both were quite excited about the adventure I was about to embark on. As the day drew to a close, my manager, being so generous, gave everyone a ten minute early mark, dependent on how quickly the farewell presentation faired. Personally, they could have skipped it and just left. I would have been thrilled. Anyway, it didn't last long at all. My manager delivered an extremely brief speech before presenting me with a second-hand Macquarie World Atlas with a new dust jacket and a travel alarm clock.

There are moments within this period I have reflected upon over the years, but I never reflected upon my employment, until now. There was one woman who stood out above the rest, a stalwart of the business. Maz was the assistant to the owner, but in all reality, she was the backbone of the place. She was an elderly woman, and I had the privilege of learning from her wisdom and experiences. Whenever I had the opportunity, I would speak with her. I'm sure she appreciated having someone she could talk with who was genuinely interested and happy to listen. I cannot remember a day when Maz wasn't full of life, including those days where she was feeling under the weather or tense. She had her own unique way of entering a room that brightened the gloomiest days, bringing smiles to the faces. She just made the day happier. Even under pressure, she never wavered.

I am sure she has long since passed, and wherever she may be, she is definitely lifting spirits and bringing smiles to faces.

Chapter 2

26th December, nineteen hundred and something. Depending on where in the world you may live…Boxing Day. I could reveal the day of the week, but that would just waste my opening line to this chapter, and I'm not about to reveal every detail. Come on, there needs to be an element of suspense and intrigue!

It was a day filled with nervous tension. On the outside, I appeared calm, but on the inside, the mind was in overdrive, over thinking, playing out every scenario imaginable. They say it's better to be prepared than the alternative. I was about to embark on a trip halfway across the world, over the Pacific, to potentially begin the next chapter of my life. There was no turning back; well…I could have if I would forego the money invested in the trip.

It is a Boxing Day that I will never forget! I was oblivious to the weather situation facing regions of the United States. States and counties endured the worst snow and ice storms they had seen in decades and that would play a role in the length of my Boxing Day. It remains the longest Boxing Day and day I have lived and I hope it remains that way, for I have no eagerness to re-live a day that seemingly never ends.

Having checked-in and passed through security (mind you, back then was a much simpler time), I made my way to the gate, spotting a seat in the corner that I could make my own, placing my carry-on in the seat next to me. Once seated, at first, I observed the people as they arrived and those merely transiting from one area to another. An airport terminal is such a melting pot of emotions…happiness, sadness, love, anxiety and more. Eventually, I turned my attention away from the people to that of the world unfolding outside the window. What seemed chaotic had an essence of organisation. To be quite frank, it was hard to remain focused with so many thoughts meandering my mind. When I refer to meandering thoughts, I truly mean meandering thoughts. I'm sure you have heard of the adage to walk a mile in another's shoes. Instead of walking a mile, spend thirty-seconds with my thoughts!

I sat alone with my thoughts, staring into the abyss. I soon snapped out of my thoughts when I noticed a stirring movement at the gate, or at least the counter. Finally, boarding would begin shortly. Well, I was sort of correct. My name bellowed across the public address system, requesting my presence at the gate. The first thought to cross my mind…this couldn't be good. Was there an issue with my booking? Reluctantly, extremely reluctantly, I grabbed my bag and ambled my way to the gate and made myself known to the staff. They were pleasant, asking if I would help a young couple. Who was I to say no? In hindsight, I should have been the one to say no. Once again, the impeccable vision of hindsight! We learn from our errors. The staff were appreciative; having exchanged seats to allow the couple to sit together.

Depending how you want to look at it, it was the romantic within me or it was simply me, making a dumb decision. If you want to debate that amongst yourselves, feel free. It wasn't much longer before the gates opened and boarding begun. Methodically, the staff shepherded the passengers through the gate and onto the plane. It still amazes me how boarding's performed in classes and sections and disembarking is a free-for-all, at least in economy! Anyhow, that is a discussion for this curious mind for another time. Having navigated through the crowded aisle to my newly assigned seat, lodging my carry-on in the overhead compartment; two elderly women made their way down the aisle. My intuition told me they would be my travelling buddies. Always trust your intuition, for it rarely leads you astray. The fact of having the two elderly women wasn't an issue overall. The only concern I had was that being in the aisle seat on a long-haul flight. I just knew this was about to be a restless and relentless up and down journey.

The flight was okay. There were a couple of patches of light turbulence, but nothing of concern. For the duration of the flight into LAX, I was up and down as predicted! Between the two women, I would say that I was up and down at least thirty or more times! I would like to say that is an embellishment, but it could actually be well under the number.

Oh yeah! For those wondering if I rested my eyes...not really. I may have dosed off and napped for a couple to a few hours at most.

The valuable lesson I discovered was to say no to a seat exchange and to make sure a window seat is available and book it.

I found some satisfaction. There is a benefit to having the aisle seat, particularly when the plane is disembarking. It still bemuses me, why people are so eager to stand in the aisle as the plane taxis and wait at length for the door to open! Anyhow, I took my time rising from my seat to then slowly stretch, as I allowed other passengers access to the overhead compartments before I fumbled my way to my bag. As the doors opened, I was standing in the limited legroom space, with my bag on my seat. I was feeling generous, so I waved through a few people before merging into the line. I am patient by nature, but even my patience can wear thin over thirteen hours.

Having left Australia in the afternoon, I arrived into LAX mid to late morning the same day. Yes, 26th December! Who said travelling through time was impossible? Everyone on that flight did it without affecting our past, present or future! I think we can all agree, we know where this chapter is heading. Being sleep deprived for some 'unknown reason', the day felt much longer.

Of course, baggage claim was fun! As I ponder all my trips, there has always been some issue. I am yet to have a clean and pleasant experience. Who knows, maybe one day it all changes. Eventually spotting my bag after forty-five minutes, I grabbed it from the conveyor. With bag in tow, I made my way to customs, where on the walk I was thinking of how this trip would unfold. Only a few more hours and I would see Dee! Without a doubt, there was a mix of excitement and nervous energy.

The queue at customs wasn't all that long, considering what I had heard about the wait times at LAX. As I was called and waved in, the customs officer greeted me with a stern tone. As he opened my passport, flipping through the pages, he asked if my trip was one of pleasure or business. Of course, I was there for pleasure and that is how I replied. I wonder how many people they catch with that question! Having explored the pages of my passport, he looked at me and asked for the address I would stay while on my visit. I gave him Dee's address and in no other terms; I was sternly informed the address supplied was not a valid address. Considering I was sleep deprived, I remained calm and explained to him that the address was that of a rural property. All mail I had sent and received was to and from that address. Without getting into specifics, the 'questioning' continued for another five minutes, although it honestly seemed much longer. The discussion continued back and forth until another officer intervened. She had her colleague explain the situation. She would apologise for the confusion, granting me entry. Finally, I was officially in the United States. Well… still in the airport.

I'm not entirely sure about the workings today, but many rural homes were yet to receive standardised addresses.

A phone card…yes, a phone card and not a SIM. Mobile phones were around. I had a Nokia, but mobile phones had yet to explode. That would be a few more years down the track, without giving too many details away! I truly was like a fish out of water, wandering the airport in search of a vending machine, a help desk or an airport concierge. After a few minutes of wandering, I stumbled upon a help desk, but keeping to the madness of my day, there was no one at the desk. I lingered in hopes someone would appear, but it wasn't my time for a miracle! Well, I wasn't about to let that small inconvenience defeat me, so I continued walking around until I found a phone card vending machine. The day was looking up! The choice in-front of me was ten, twenty, or fifty-dollar cards, so I opted for the fifty. I pulled a crisp fifty-dollar note from my wallet, lined it up with the intake on the vending machine and fed it in until the rollers grabbed the note. You know what is coming next! Half of the note disappeared before being rejected. It wasn't anything of concern, just a little frustrating. Before feeding the note again, I looked at the orientation instructions, verifying I had fed it correctly the first time. Once more, I fed the note as it disappeared into the mechanical workings. Upon entering the associated code, I waited for the card to drop. Nothing! I mean nothing! There wasn't a movement nor an audible indication. I pressed the code once more and waited in vain. Fifty-dollars had just gone south! With no help desk operational, I had to concede…fifty-dollars lost and the day just continuing to drag out! In my frustration, I gave the machine a quick and aggressive shake, to no avail! Before leaving on the trip, Dee provided me with the reverse charges number, but I had no plans to utilise it. Even the best laid plans can quickly turn into disarray!

With the fiasco now behind me, or what I could only hope was behind me, I would trudge along to make my connecting flight. First, I did not know where the domestic terminal was, but I trusted myself to figure it out. As the sliding doors opened, I stepped outside for the first time. The day was bright and warm; glancing left to stare down the long straight pathway, and then looking right to see a mirror image. It was a flip of the coin moment. My gut was leaning right, so right I went. Along my walk, I came across an airport police officer, whom I asked for directions. He was quite polite; reassuring me I was heading in the right direction and that it wasn't all too far. The first terminal doors I would come across would be the terminal. I was appreciative and thanked him and continued on my journey. Some five minutes of walking later, I arrived at the terminal, well…sort of? It was an entrance, at least. Passing through the doors, the area was without a soul, and the luggage conveyor to the left remained motionless. I was wondering if I was in the right spot! The terminal should be bustling with people. Part curiosity and the rest, "no way in hell is this day going to get any worse" led me to explore the area. I would notice a wall that appeared oddly out of place, well, at least to me. I ventured further around to find a narrow staircase. Climbing the stairs, the sound of life reverberated and upon reaching the top, a whole new world was awaiting, a terminal bustling!

Wasting no further time, I made a B-Line to the information monitors, searching for my flight. I would eventually locate it, and the word CANCELLED prominently featured beside it. Yeah…some more human interaction as I made my way to the airline counter, politely asking about the current situation and the options available. Be aware, this was my first solo travels, so I was learning everything on the go. The young woman took the time to explain the current weather back east and the chaotic domino effect it had. After referring to the system, collecting my details, she confirmed my re-scheduled flight for the following morning and I need not do a thing. Apologising for the inconvenience, which I can only imagine was a regular phrase for her that day. She then pointed me in the direction of the hotel courtesy phones where I could organise a room for the night. Yes, I know what many of you are thinking; it was the airline's responsibility to provide a room for the night. They provided me with vouchers for the room and a meal for a specific hotel chain. Anyhow, little did I realise how difficult this would be, with flights being cancelled left, right and centre during the busiest time of year, Thanksgiving through New Year. At first, no rooms were available at the Marriott, but the receptionist gave me the heads up, letting me know to call after six. She explained the situation and added me to a reserve list or something similar that would offer me a bit of security regarding my chances of securing an available room. It was nice of her to help, but I also had to trust blindly as well, which isn't the easiest of things to do.

Needing to occupy myself for a few hours. I found a quiet spot, as quiet as it got in a busy terminal. Having propped myself against a wall, I pulled out a pen and notebook and penned several pieces in the time. For the curious, those pieces penned will never see the light of day.

For those wondering why I didn't opt to explore. It was only a few hours at most, and I wasn't about to lug around two bags.

A couple of minutes before six, I picked myself up, made my way to the courtesy phones. To be honest, I wasn't confident, expecting that I would have to bunker down for the night in the terminal. With a stroke of fortune, the receptionist was still on duty and there were a couple of cancellations. Without wasting a further breath, I grabbed the room. Maybe, just maybe, my luck was now about to change! The receptionist also provided me directions to locate the designated pickup zone for the shuttle.

To finally arrive at the Marriott, albeit, quite late, I was relieved, making my way to reception and checking in. I noticed I was the only passenger. The other four being pilots and cabin crew. Check-in was a breeze, and having made my way to my room, dropping off my bags, I quickly splashed water on my face before heading down to the eatery. I didn't feel hungry, but my stomach would disagree judging by the strange sounds emanating from its depths! Coincidentally, the pilots and cabin crew arrived virtually at the same time. From the appearance of the floor, the bar was the only area open. To all our disappointments, the kitchen had closed for the evening, but like I assumed, the bar, still open. I ordered myself a lemonade and sat at the farthest end, facing the only access in or out. As I sat there drinking my lemonade, I hoped that come tomorrow, all this misfortune would be a thing of the past...an isolated incident. As I did then, I still find it difficult to believe of the events that unfolded that day. Knowing the staff would like to call it a night, I quickly finished my drink to retire to my room. Along the way, I caught sight of a vending machine tucked away in a recessed area. Yes, I rolled the dice this time; my stomach had become quite restless and relentless. However, I was only prepared to sacrifice a five-dollar note.

I can feel the suspense...you are wondering if the machine devoured my donation or upped the ante and had the coil wind prematurely, to only dangle the item; mocking me. Well, it was neither! The machine gladly accepted the note and released the selected item, where the sound of a thud on the tray below was comforting. My fortunes had to be turning, undeniably, when I received change! Not even the universe could play such an elaborate prank, or could it? I contemplated purchasing another snack, but I wasn't about to push my luck!

Continuing towards my room, I remembered seeing a row of payphones. Taking the opportunity, I called Dee. I knew it was early in the east, but I also knew she would appreciate the call. I dialled the reverse charges number and she picked-up and accepted quickly. We were both relieved to hear one another's voices. I let her know of the cancellation and the rescheduling and that I would arrive a day later than planned. It elated her to know I was in the country and it wouldn't be long now. I would like to say that I shared the same elation, but I was so tired, I just wanted to sleep, even if only for a few hours. It doesn't mean I wasn't excited; I was! Before ending the call, I told her that by this time tomorrow, we would be together. SPOILER ALERT: remember how I mentioned I thought my luck was turning? Well…you'll just have to continue reading. Having hung-up with Dee, I returned to my room and crashed into the armchair. Hey, when you are exhausted, anywhere is fine!

With a couple of stray rays of sunlight finding the gaps between the curtains, a new day was born. I wasn't about to leave anything further to chance or to the infamous Murphy. I grabbed a shower, checked-out, minus breakfast and made my way directly to the airport, with more than enough time to spare! It was a new day, a new beginning; everything would get back on track and flow to plan! Ha! Who the hell was I kidding?

Returning to the airport, I was astonished to see the crowd! I was expecting the traffic to be heavy, but I conceived nothing like this! It took me at least thirty minutes to navigate my way into the terminal and to the end of the queue for my flight, or so I believed. However, I was a little confused, for my flight was a direct flight and this was now making a stop in St Louis? Ahead of me, an elderly couple who struck up a conversation. It was quite an interesting conversation, having learnt much of their lives and the trials and tribulations of their children. I opened up slightly, explaining the reason for being in the US. The wife thought it to be romantic and hoped for a wonderful outcome. As the conversation lengthened, the queue—moving nowhere. I asked if I was in the right queue and I was. Because of the cancellations, flights now doubled up, where direct flights would now have a stop-over to help ease the demand on the airlines. Before the conversation could flow further, the husband, without missing a beat, told me that if I remained in the queue, likely I would spend another night in LA. He told me to use the kerbside check-in. He explained to leave a generous tip and that once I had checked in; I would receive a receipt of confirmation. I was to go directly to the gate and hand the receipt to the staff, where a boarding pass would be printed. They told me to go and wished me all the best. That couple left an impression on me. They didn't have to help a stranger, but they did. Following his instructions. I was able to make the flight. I received my boarding pass as boarding had begun. To my amazement, I was in First-Class. I would say the term 'First-Class' was liberal. The seats appeared average and were not all inviting regarding comfortability. There was leg room, and that's a positive in my book. Honestly, what would I know about First-Class? This was my first adventure flying First-Class.

As the plane awaited clearance, I reflected on the kindness of that couple and if I happened not to cross paths, would I have made the flight? Would I be stuck in LA? What if this was a message from the universe? I will never know the answers. I am extremely grateful that my path intersected with them.

Kindness still exists; you just need to keep your eyes open.

The flight departed on time and, from all reports, scheduled to arrive in St Louis on time. This would be the beginning of another wild and adventurous ride!

Chapter 3

Somewhere high in the skies above the western United States, I was relatively comfortable in the seat; after all, it is an aircraft seat! My flying companion was a junior executive of an up-and-coming business that continues to flourish today. She was heading back east for some business, but to also reunite with family and friends. We chatted about her trip home and how the weather created utter chaos for thousands of people trying to either re-unite with family or to return home. Eventually, the topic shifted onto me, something I was avoiding, but I knew I wouldn't be able to prevent it. Maybe if it was a shorter flight. I spoke of my writings, how I thought the genre was now relegated to a niche market and that of the trip to a discrete extent. It was enjoyable chatting with her and before either of us knew; we were on approach to St Louis. How could I not resist peering out the window; greeted with the sight of the mighty Mississippi snaking across the landscape as it shimmered in the afternoon light.

As the plane touched down, taxiing to the gate, passengers continuing on to New York, reminded to remain seated. This is what I like to refer as the 'Chaotic Transfer'. To keep myself occupied, I watched the ground crew at work, removing the luggage to load into the trailers. I noticed my bag in one trailer. My bag was quite distinct, and the odds of another on the same flight would have likely been out of this world. Regardless, my bag was driven off into the sunset and there wasn't a thing I could do, but watch in disbelief. Apparently, my luck hadn't changed and my bag decided it needed a separate vacation. I just hoped that it would be waiting for me when I landed in New York, but I was far from confident that it would still be in the country. Who says travelling isn't stressful?

You wouldn't conceive it could get much worse, right? Wrong! Somehow, I think the spirit of Murphy was having far too much fun at my expense to stop just yet. As I briefly digress…how I wish I could travel through time, for I would make sure Murphy's parents never met! Murphy has not only caused trouble and frustration for me, but for many a person over the years.

With the cabin crew boarding for the New York leg, they were less than happy; yet quite chirpy to air their grievances publicly. What I deciphered from the choice selection of words and tonality, either there was a dispute brewing or it could have been ongoing between the cabin crew and the pilots. If I were to transcribe the chatter, much would be redacted! There was no love lost between the rival parties. The situation heightened when the pilots had yet to appear. Emotions were on high and there was a discussion, followed by an active threat of walking off the plane if they failed to show within the next fifteen minutes. It was about this point; I was thinking I must be in a nightmare. Fortunately, calmer heads prevailed, and the pilots appeared within the fifteen minutes.

What appeared to be a promising day, at least compared to the previous day, surely snowballed into something I can only describe as agonising.

With the layover and industrial action, the flight ended up being delayed. To add insult to injury, take-off was aborted due to an apparent engine issue. There was no chance I was making the connecting flight. The plane remained on the tarmac while the crew investigated the issue. On-board, the passengers became restless, as well as the cabin crew. Eventually, the booming voice of the captain echoed through the cabin, informing the passengers of the issue having been resolved and that we'd be taking off shortly and making up time! Okay, making up time? How the hell does an aircraft make up hours of lost time without the assistance of a cyclonic tail wind?

It was a relatively long and tiresome flight. Unlike Missouri, there really wasn't much to see. The abysmal weather prevented the bright lights of Manhattan from making any impact. Was I disappointed, no. I just wanted the plane to make its final approach, land and that would bring another set of problems to deal with, another day featuring more of the same, but another step closer to Dee.

Having disembarked, there was no need for me to venture to the carousel. Instead, I made my way to the service desk, where greeted by a young woman. To begin, I addressed the obvious of missing my connecting flight. Well, the young woman then informed me the flight had departed hours ago and I should have been at the airport prior to departure. Apparently, when I explained the situation to begin, she either was selective with the information she heard or she didn't listen to a single word. As frustrated and infuriated as I was, I remained level-headed and explained the entire situation once more, pausing at length and intervals. She quickly apologised for the inconvenience and quick to search and organise the next available flight. After a moment, she looked me dead in the eye and told me there was a flight out tonight, the last for the evening, from La Guardia in thirty-minutes. I, being a New York Yankee fan and interested in geography, had become familiar with New York. There was no way in hell I could make it unless teleportation technology existed! Therefore, I asked her if she thought I would make the flight, which she promptly replied with a no way. I remained calm and polite, although I was ready to erupt on the inside. I simply gave her a look. She informed me of tomorrow's first available flight, being an early afternoon departure. Okay, some progress. Now it was a matter of accommodation for the night; receiving a complimentary room and a meal voucher for use at the Hilton.

Having thanked her, I asked about the location of the lost baggage office. Without missing a beat, she asked me why I needed the lost baggage office. I don't know, because I just wanted to know. However, I didn't say that. I explained my bag did not arrive and left it at that. She would point me in the right direction.

The lost luggage office offered as much fun! The guy at the service counter possessed the most unenthusiastic voice I've encountered. He asked if I was reporting or collecting. Having informed him I was there to report, he handed me a form and told me to fill it out. Looking over the form, I thought I was reporting a missing person with the amount of detail required; from colour, shape, size, pattern, material, zippers, zipper style, wheels, handles, straps, locks, labels and items within the bag. Who else was the airline planning to involve in the search?

Having managed not to erupt, I now needed to find the hotel shuttle. Arriving at the stop, I was confused and shocked. Waiting was a coach, not a shuttle like in LA. I wasn't the only one perplexed, with the guy in-front being hesitant; approaching the door, he asked the driver and was assured it was the Hilton shuttle. What did I have to lose…maybe winding up in another city? The driver seemed somewhat in a hurry, departing with his foot to the floor, reminding me of some of the bus drivers experienced during my school years. Coming to a stop was also an exciting moment, where he would try to stop on a dime! The driver pushed his luck one too many times, having caught the eye of the New York City Police. While stopped at traffic lights, a patrol car rolled up alongside. The driver opened the coach door and after a few seconds, I clearly heard a verbal tirade. With the changing of the lights and possibly a stroke of fortune, the door closed and the coach pulled away with the patrol car continuing on with their duties; I assume. When I look back, I feel if the lights hadn't changed at that moment, the tirade would have escalated to a point of no return!

By the time I checked-in and made my way to my room, a new day was beginning as the clock passed midnight. Upon opening the door, it didn't take all that long for me to crash. The stress and exhaustion were taking a toll on my body.

Come the morning, I was up early to freshen up, grabbed some breakfast with the meal voucher, and checked out early. After LA, I wasn't about to leave anything further to chance, so if it meant hanging around the airport longer, so be it!

An early arrival at the airport and I found a relatively isolated seat. As usual, to bide my time, people watching mostly. I did, from time to time, monitor the weather through the window. Looking out onto the runways, it was clear how much snow had fallen as the grounds crew piled the snow cleared to the sides of the runways. Up to that point in my life, I had never seen so much snow. The patchy blue skies were deteriorating. With the trip so far, it would seem appropriate that the weather take a turn for the worst. Either the flight would depart as scheduled or I would be stuck in New York for an undetermined period.

However, Murphy just couldn't leave it at the threat of weather. Oh no! An uneasy-looking guy ambled in to take the seat opposite to me. There were plenty of other empty seats, but why he chose that seat, I wonder! After he settled into his seat, he acted out, and it wasn't long before airport security was on the scene. With security, the man became agitated, sending him into what I would call an unnerving state, bordering on frenzied. There I was, in the proverbial box seat as security spoke with the guy, before leaving him to his own devices. The guy acted out more, verbally and physically; unsettling many having since arrived. It wasn't too long before the New York Police arrived on the scene with paramedics in tow. Security met the officers, had a brief discussion before making their way into the terminal. As they approached, he started lashing out and screaming. What he was screaming was inaudible to me. The officers restrained him, controlling the situation, having restrained him on the ground, and thus allowing the paramedics to perform their duties. Eventually, he would be escorted from the terminal in cuffs, much to the relief of everyone present. When I look back on the situation, I can't but help to think how fortunate everyone was. The situation had the potential to escalate rapidly, and no one knew if he was carrying a concealed weapon, either. Remember, this was a time before security of today.

Everyone could now breathe somewhat easier and focus their attention on the weather and flight.

Speaking of the weather, it had considerably deteriorated to earlier. The wind whipping with strong and variable gusts and a light dusting of snow had fallen, a prelude to the flurries around the corner. I was waiting to hear the announcement of the flight's cancellation over the PA. The PA came alive, but rather than announce the cancellation of the flight, the announcement was for the commencement of boarding. I could say it again, maybe a turning point! I think we all have learnt, this trip wasn't meant to be smooth sailing!

Exiting the comfortable warmth of the terminal and into the teeth of the frigid New York air, where the wind cut to the bone! To be out on the tarmac and to have a better view of the snow piled up, it made me realise the significance of the weather event and how challenging it must be for all involved. Excluding the pilot and co-pilot, our numbers totalled that of six. Yep, six passengers, and yet I couldn't conceive what the other five passengers must have experienced to this point. Boarding the twin rotary engine plane was a tad challenging, having to remember to remain hunched throughout boarding. Being tall brings its own set of challenges. Once everyone was aboard and seated, the engines came to life! The props spinning and the unmistakable sound of a sputtering engine reverberating throughout the cabin. The little engine that could, now on its advance as the cabin rocked and rolled.

Let's just say, the little engine that could and the weather inspired little confidence. The plane somehow managed to get airborne and once at altitude, the chatter on the plane was how everyone came to be in this situation. Most stranded since Christmas and a couple, stranded since Thanksgiving! That's crazy, considering Thanksgiving falls on the last Thursday of November. Only a person lacking empathy and compassion could not feel for these people.

Oh, the little engine that could. How would I describe it? Hmm...how does a sardine tin, but only slightly roomier sound? The dividing wall between the cabin and cockpit was flimsy. A hearty sneeze could have knocked down the wall. Not only was it flimsy, it was paper thin; conversations in the cockpit were audible, even adding the sound of the sputtering engines. Basically, there were no secrets between us.

About half an hour or maybe more from our destination in Richmond, when we noticed the reduction in volume of the pilot and co-pilots chatter. Any respected person knows when someone lowers their voice; there is an attempt to conceal information. The co-pilot soon emerged to inform us of the deteriorating conditions in Richmond, and the airport was now closed to all traffic and the plane would divert back to JFK. A collective sigh of disappointment filled the cabin, understandably why. These people experienced hell to just get home, and here they were with another hiccup to deal with. Although disappointed, they weren't broken! It's truly amazing how resilient people can be and yet we all have our breaking points. With the co-pilot retiring to the cockpit, the plane would bank and start the return journey to JFK. Within five minutes of breaking the news of Richmond, the co-pilot re-emerged to break further bad news, with JFK now closed to all traffic. The next point of call on this trip was Dulles. As you probably can guess, that option wasn't on the table for long as the pilot yelled out the closure of Dulles. The next airport of choice, or probably the only one still open, Baltimore. A couple of questions meandered my mind, the first being will it remain open and the other being, does the plane have enough fuel?

As you guessed, Baltimore would close, leaving us with the tiniest of opportunities to land in Washington D.C. We tightened our buckles, crossed our fingers and made a run for the airport, knowing at any moment, air traffic control would likely close the airport due to the intense weather system and deteriorating conditions.

With heavy winds and what I assume cross winds, the plane, thrown about like a rag doll. Looking out the windows, visibility was zero as torrential rain obscured all vision. With the plane making its final approach, you could feel the immense impact of the winds. The little engine that could was taking a beating, and yet was holding together, but how much could it endure? As the plane descended, the pilot was in a bitter battle with Mother Nature...the rear wheels touching down on the flooded tarmac before hydroplaning or aquaplaning, depending on which term you prefer. On board, it felt as if we were aboard a ferry in turbulent seas, before the pilot gained control and balanced out the plane as the front-wheel touched down. With all wheels on the ground, the wind gusts were relentlessly trying to push the little engine that could over; failing to succeed.

What the pilot and I assume co-pilot accomplished in the worst conditions I have encountered to date was just unbelievable! There were moments where all passengers felt the plane would inevitably flip, and yet it didn't, coming to a stop as the sound of the deluge outside dominated over the sound of the twin engines. The door opened, the wind angry, howling as the rain sweeping in sheets, parallel to the ground!

Disembarking was hell! Trying to navigate the few stairs was the first challenge. Navigating the conditions to get across the tarmac and into the safety of the terminal was the next challenge. The ferocity of the rain made it difficult to see. The flooded tarmac added further difficulties. Trying to remain upright required every ounce of strength. There were moments when the wind managed to get the better of me, pushing me back, but I relented to push forward and into the safety of the terminal. Once inside, there wasn't a dry soul amongst us.

Appreciating the efforts of the pilot and co-pilot, we expressed our gratitude with an offer to buy them a meal. Referring to company policy; they declined the offer and continued to work to get us to our destination in Richmond.

Three quarters of an hour passed, and the pilot re-emerged with bad news. Richmond and JFK would not be re-opening before tomorrow afternoon at earliest based on future weather forecasts and the airline would not be running any flights until further notice, effectively leaving us high and dry (well, not so much dry). Someone asked of the possibility of compensation, accommodation and/or a meal voucher. The pilot informed us the airline would not be making such offers. The pilots, being far from impressed with head office and management, guaranteed to find us a way into Richmond that night. It was considerate of them and something they didn't have to do. They would secure a shuttle bus that would complete the last leg of the journey. Officially, I know not of who paid for the shuttle, but I can have a good guess! A couple of remarkable guys who proved humanity still exists.

Well, it looked like everyone was to make their final destination. I would never have thought I would arrive, or should I say, landing at the airport on a shuttle bus rather than a plane.

The wind had since eased and the rain had calmed to showers. The luggage loaded onto the shuttle and, from my calculations, an extra bag made its way onboard. Let's just say someone was about to have a misfortunate evening and a lesson, not to leave your bags unattended and amongst a large group of bags. Once arriving in Richmond, the bag would surely find its way back to its owner. At least, I hoped.

The drive wasn't anything spectacular. I glimpsed the White House in the distance and the red strobe high upon the Washington Monument. The rest was like any other city or large town at night in the rain.

Arriving in Richmond and the airport, we said our goodbyes as we headed off in our respective directions, for what we hoped to be an unobstructed journey home. I wonder what happened to those on the plane…I hope they found fortune in their lives. After what they endured, each deserved it.

Entering through the furthest arrivals door, I had a quick glance in the near vicinity, but didn't see Dee. As I scanned further abroad; spotting her walking towards me from the opposite end. Judging by her body language, she had yet to see me. It didn't take long before our eyes connected. We hugged in a relieving embrace and kissed. She was a little more enthusiastic than me, for I was beyond fatigued. Finally, the crazy adventure, over!

As we exited the airport to make our way to her car, Dee explained how her friend provided her with access to the radio broadcast, eavesdropping on the plans discussed by air traffic control and the pilot. She was well aware of everything that unfolded and even commenting to her friend to relay a message to the pilot; instructing him to throw a parachute on me, push me out and relay the co-ordinates so she could collect me. A parachute! Hey now! There is no need for me to be jumping out of a perfectly working aircraft! Just in that moment, I could see the passion within her, as well as the frustration, stress and tiredness. Exhausted, I wasn't all that talkative and Dee understood. She just wanted to get us home, but needed to make a stop to fill up the tank.

For the past week, power had been out, so life was operating at a bare minimum. It was the worst ice storm seen in decades and current reports had nearby counties establishing grid re-connections, which was great! Approaching the service station, I noticed what looked to be of tape, stretched across one side of the building and the other end to a bowser. As we drove up the drive, it became apparent it was police tape. Dee commented there must have been a fatality, likely a robbery, as she pointed out three bullet holes in the window. Well, my first international crime scene. I cannot say this trip lacked excitement!

Dee would find another service station to fill up before heading home.

Over the years, I've referred to that moment being our first date. How could you top such a moment? Flying halfway across the world, hampered by severe weather, landing at an airport by bus and being introduced to the darker side of any nation…a crime scene.

Approaching what I would call home for the next few months, the bitumen continued to sweep to the right, but for us, the road to the left was that of a gravel track. Apart from the beam of the headlights, the only visible light was that of the houses, tucked back from the road and behind the tree line. The city was a distant memory as we headed deep into the countryside and the woods. This was the back country, where deer and snakes were as common as squirrel stew. It was also the ideal location for a horror movie! This part of the country wouldn't be favourable to anyone who feared the dark. About halfway down the gravel track, Dee pulled up and into the drive, briefly illuminating what looked to be a single-storey house built somewhere around the forties or fifties. Once out of the car and allowing for the eyes to adjust, trees surrounded the front of the property and, from the gutters, icicles ominously dangled. As the wind gusted through the bare and icy tree branches; an eerie sound echoed. It is difficult to describe, but it sounded brittle and chilling. Again, ideal for a horror movie setting!

Upon entering the house, Dee reached out and flicked the light switch on the wall. The filament in the globe flickered before slowly illuminating brighter. Power restored! However, there was no running water. Being out in the countryside, properties weren't connected to town water as referred to in the States, rather well water. Each property had a well, and that well required a pump. With power restored, the pump required priming, something left to the hours of sunlight. Nobody wants to be lying on the frozen ground, dangling their arm into a dark pit, unable to see what surprise may wait! We were both exhausted anyway. She showed me to our room, where we both crashed as soon as our heads hit the pillows. There could have been a tornado siren screeching, and I would have been none the wiser until I awoke the following morn.

Chapter 4

Opening my eyes that next morning was amazing on many levels. The morning light, shimmering as it penetrated between the curtains to illuminate the room. Wiping the sleep from my eyes, turning my head to see Dee next to me, her arm draped across my chest. I absorbed the moment; watching her as she slept; no thought for the previous days, just living the moment and allowing myself to wander into the future. I wasn't able to sleep watch for too long as she begun stirring, wrapping herself around me, as the sunlight enticed her eyes open. The realisation was clear, with a smile across her face, followed by a soft, good morning. For the next hour, we lay there cuddling and enjoying the moment. What we had been longing and craving for was finally here!

Eventually, and somewhat reluctantly, we needed to get out of bed. After a quick bite for breakfast, I asked Dee to point me to the well. Out front, an inconspicuous round concrete slab, where I raised the cover. Dee wandered to the other side of the house to open the spigot. After some stretching and manoeuvring, I had my hands on the pump. It wasn't long before I had it primed. In the distance; the sound of air rushing through the pipes ahead of the imminent surge. Running water and a hot shower loomed! It seems so trivial, but after all the delays and the lost luggage, it was a win, and as they say, a win is a win.

A hot shower…to feel that soothing water falling from the shower rose, cascading as it washed away the tension and events of the previous days. I could have stayed under the shower all day, but we had plans to visit the local mall for a spot of clothes shopping, for me of course as I did not know when or if my bag would arrive from its impromptu vacation!

The air was still and somewhat brisk. The skies were cloudless, and there was a distinctive freshness to the late morning air. Something you don't experience in the city or suburbs. The trip along the interstate was smooth and orderly, quite different from Australian freeways and motorways. We chatted about everything and yet nothing in particular. We were in the moment, enjoying one another's company. The chat eventually gave way to singing; the staple of any road trip. For me to sing, either I'm extremely comfortable or I'm in love. Rarely does either happen; so on this occasion, it was a rarity, with comfort and love being prominent. Anyhow, Dee and I shared a passion for the classics, where lyrics were meaningful and stimulating and the music composed was of beauty and there was none of this auto-tune bullshit!

The mall…one of the largest in the south. I believe it still exists today, but I'm sure we can no longer refer to it as one of the largest. The car park was the size of a small city. Concrete and glass with large signs everywhere. People hustling and bustling, pounding the concrete with intent. Never had I seen or encountered anything equivalent in Australia.

Inside, as impressive as the outside, a city within a city. Mind you, a well-designed city. It didn't take long to find the stores and to purchase what I needed.

Dee needed to stock up on a few groceries; therefore, a quick minute drive across the car park brought us to the Food Lion, a supermarket chain. I'm relatively confident the chain still exists...I could be mistaken. Nope. A quick search and I can confirm it still exists.

During my time, I would visit another two Food Lion stores in different counties and there is something they all share in common...and no, not the name of the company or logo! Each store featured the exact layout from aisles, to specials and to item placements. Laugh if you must, but at the second store, as I walked into the car park, I needed to stop for a minute to gather my bearings. It is difficult to describe without having experienced the situation. Dee noticed my pause and laughed before letting me know I wasn't the first and definitely wouldn't be the last to be deceived.

After that slight detour, the trip home seemed quicker. I think we've all experienced such a moment where the initial trip to a new place seems longer. With the sun slowly dipping lower in the western sky, the shadows outstretching across the landscape and the colours of the sky morphing into vivid hues; we veered from the interstate and onto the back roads. Farmland adorned either side. Some fields prepped and awaiting to be sewn. As we approached a sweeping bend, Dee pointed out a particular farm and explained how, a few years earlier, the owner built a rental house on the outer portion of the property. Farmers in the area were experiencing financial woes, so any financial gain would offer relief. The farmer rented out the house to a family who ended up losing their lives; executed. Each member of the family found with their hands bound behind them and a single bullet wound to the rear of their heads. Quite a shocking dose of reality! Like most small towns, the rumours had the family, or at least the adults involved in the drug scene. The execution, either a message or they screwed over the wrong people. Usually, country rumours are more factual than rumour. Those responsible had yet to be apprehended and possibly never have.

A mile further down the road, the farmland suddenly transformed into dense woods. Being in a wooded area and near farmland, it wasn't uncommon to hear a rifle or shotgun echoing across the airwaves. With hunters and farmers alike, the sound of a gunshot wouldn't draw much attention. During my stay, I can recall countless occasions where I heard shots echo out. It was unsettling at first, considering the different culture of Australia and the United States, but I acclimated with time. With Dee's help, I was able to distinguish between the different weapons fired.

The sun's light was drastically waning as we arrived home; I could see ever the pale beam of the headlights illuminating the siding of the house. That brief illumination highlighted a surprise! On the porch waiting, my missing luggage. I did not know how long it had been there, but I can guarantee that if it was in the city or suburbs, I likely wouldn't have known the airline delivered it until I chased it up. Fortunately, there are benefits to being so isolated. I was glad to have my luggage back in my possession.

I wouldn't say the following week was less active, as it was productive. We used the week to explore our desires and to familiarise ourselves. We were in our world, and yet co-existing with the natural world that seemed stuck between the determination of winter and the wistful will of spring. Most mornings were brisk and sunny, gradually warming as the day aged. There were days that provided a glimpse of the spring to be, only to transform into the bitterly cold evenings of winter.

There were many days that stood out, but one truly shone. As I sit behind the keys typing, I'm watching the video of that day for the first time in years. The memories...I'm transported back to that single moment; the sights, the sounds, and the scents come flooding back.

It was a grey and yet a bright day. Snow flurries persisted throughout the morning before easing in the afternoon, only to pick up once more in the early hours of the evening. Dee; required to run some errands, so with the camcorder already in hand and rolling, I documented our brief foray. As we drove past the only traffic sign, Dee explained the interesting historical parts of the town. Noticeably, there were no traffic lights and but a solitary stop sign. Come to think of it, a give way (yield) sign would have sufficed considering the location and traffic. Within the city limits, two churches, a post office (established 1908); a couple of now defunct businesses and a general store that once served as a petrol/gas station. The bowsers remained in place. If I would have a guess, they looked to be from the mid to late 80s. The general store was also the central hub...the pulse of the town. I will talk more of that later. Unfortunately, it no longer exists. That came as quite a shock! An empty lot is all that remains, but that may have changed in recent years. It is saddening to know the general store; a piece of history is now gone.

The outskirts, and where you find the local rubbish tip. Rubbish tip might be misleading. In Australia, we hear rubbish tip and picture an enormous hole in the ground. The tip comprised of two large shipping containers converted into commercial/industrial style bins.

After a quick trip to the post office, next on the agenda was the tip! Just a quick drive down the road; to the right, farmland and to the left, dense woods featuring a small cut-out. There was enough real estate for three cars to park, but in reality, who was parking? In the dead of winter, the smell was horrendous; you can only imagine the stench in the heat of summer! As of its existence; a couple of years ago, it remained in operation and hadn't changed in appearance.

On our return, we stopped at the general store. Dee was excited for me to experience the atmosphere of a typical country store. The stairs and landing, constructed of salvaged wood, a throwback and homage to a bygone era, an era where you fell or recycled the wood required. It revealed distinct hand tool markings, which added charm! Upon pulling the door open, a small brass bell rung aloud. Let me just say, the bell didn't go unnoticed! To the right, the counter and register and for the floor layout itself, a few shelves scattered. Towards the rear of the store and slightly off-centred was that of a blackened pot-belly stove. The glow of the flames illuminating the open vents. On top, a cast-iron coffee pot warming, similar to those we've all seen in the movies, especially those with a Western theme.

Positioned around the stove, hand-crafted pieces of oak and hickory that served as bench seating. Seated on said benches, the local farmers. Remember how I mentioned when the bell rung, it didn't go unnoticed? On our approach to the door, the chattering voices of the farmers clearly heard. As soon as I placed one foot inside the store, their voices fell silent; as they fixed all eyes on me, the strange man that I somehow believe knew of my arrival before I arrived in the country. For the duration of our visit, with Dee picking a few pieces to at least cover-up the true reason of our visit, the farmers remained silent, keeping a watchful eye as they drank their freshly brewed coffee.

I still can envision the moment and it continues to bring a smile to my face.

Once home, Dee would share further insight into the farmers and how they headed into the general store to share advice, knowledge and to complain. But really, they enjoyed their gossip! How I would have loved to be a fly on the wall after I left!

Just a few days later, the weather changed once more. Predominantly blue skies featuring scattered clouds. The mercury was on the rise, warmer temperatures accompanied by a gentle breeze blowing from the south-west. Spring was outstretching its influence over the bitter chill of winter. With it being such a lovely day, we jumped at the opportunity to get out of the house and take a stroll along the old mill pond. Walking hand in hand, Dee described how the mill had operated until the early part of the twentieth century. I love history, and not only was I fascinated with what she had to say, I was enjoying just being near her. As we walked around the pond, she would point out the hidden remnants of the mill, making sure I was also aware of the possibility of an encounter with a Water Moccasin, also known as Cottonmouths. For those unaware, Water Moccasins are venomous. With the weather warming, there was a greater possibility of activity. Better safe than sorry. Continuing along, she pointed out lesser known battlegrounds of the Civil

War, which I found amazing! I was unaware these grounds existed. She would spot the many Native American arrowheads scattered along the path. The arrowheads seamlessly blended in with the rocks and stones.

The walk was lovely, fuelled by the scenery, the history and, of course, the company of the woman beside me.

With the day ageing and the weather cooling, it was time to return. The walk back provided an alternative view to the mill, revealing further decaying remnants of its structure. It wouldn't be much longer before nature would reclaim the remnants and a part of history lost forever. Still, I was fortunate to see a significant part of the area's history. I could picture the massive logs floating upon the water when the mill was at the height of its production. I couldn't help to wonder how many logs may still exist, resting beneath the waters of the pond. While in my state of daydreaming, Dee was quick to point out a Cottonmouth sunning itself in a small open area, only a few metres from us.

Finally home, the sun setting and the air having more of a brisk feel, it was time to clean up branches and a few leaves, once frozen in time. Yes, there were a few leaves. Mostly, it was small branches and twigs that had snapped during the ice storm. With the warmer weather, the surface thaw had begun. Albeit, the ground, still quite frozen. Dee asked me to grab the rake from the shed, reminding me to make myself known before entering. "Make myself known. What, was there an entity residing in there?"...She quickly pointed out there could be snakes making the shed home, and not uncommon for them to be anywhere, including above the door. Wonderful! Well, there was no way I was about to walk into the shed unannounced! I announced my presence! Every soul in the vicinity heard me thumping and shaking the shed. I do need to say, the construction of the shed was impeccable.

Unlatching the door with a large branch in hand, pushing it open before poking the branch around the door frame, making sure I had ample distance for any falling surprises. For the sake of my luck, nothing fell from above and that was a relief! Venturing in, still mindful, and alert to any movement or snake-like shapes. The rake, hanging on the rear wall; however what caught my attention was that of an immense piece of canvas. Clearly, it was covering something significant. Being curious, I had a quick look and was surprised at what I saw. Having the glimpse, I grabbed the rake and headed out. As I began raking the debris into a pile, I mentioned to Dee of what I saw. She hid nothing, telling me that the copper pot I saw was a still. Now, that caught my attention, was Dee a shiner and/or bootlegger! No, she wasn't. However, it belonged to someone known to her and since passed away. They weren't bootleggers, but they were moonshiners. This trip was becoming more and more interesting as it progressed. To her understanding, they produced the moonshine for personal consumption, and from my understanding, state law allowed for x amount to be distilled for personal use. Albeit, that was a massive still and no one would believe that still was for personal consumption. It was intriguing, if I am to be honest. I had heard and read about moonshiners and bootleggers. This is well before the series came to air and bringing popularity to a larger audience. I knew of the basic principles and recipe, though recipes vary and are sacred, traditionally passed down to those trusted.

I would have loved the opportunity to have sat down with both a shiner and bootlegger and listened to their stories and of their experiences.

Back to raking. Dee dragged across an old steel bin, placing it on a line of bare and blackened earth. It was perfect timing, as the sun's light now filtered through the bare branches of the woods. The bitter chill of the night air, settling. Having piled the debris, we scooped it into the bin where Dee set it alight. Just the sight of the flames rising from the depths and the crackling sound provided a warming sensation. It wasn't long before the radiant heat from the flames could be appreciated. There we stood, holding each other, watching the flames dance above the rim. It might not sound like much, but it was a simple and yet wonderful moment.

The simplest of actions possess the most meaning and love.

Before the last light extinguished, a small Cottonmouth arose from the earth near the hot bin, to make its way into the nearby woods and to safety.

That evening, we enjoyed in the romance and indulged ourselves with a couple of movies. That night was tough to sleep as I remember. Hey now, your thoughts are way off the track. Just keep reading.

Dee's neighbour shared the same surname as a neighbour from a well-known sitcom of the time. Some of you may work it out.

Her neighbour owned a rooster, a rooster that just hadn't understood the concept of time that we use and apparently had become extremely fond of a shrub beneath the bedroom window. The rooster would make himself known during the wee hours of the morning, and when I refer to wee hours, I mean between the hours of two and three. Mind you, it wasn't a regular occurrence either. Come to think of it, I never heard the rooster at any time between the hours of five and midday. I have my suspicions…Murphy!

Chapter 5

Dee was a unique woman. Compassionate, warm, empathetic, passionate, determined, strong, intelligent, humorous and flowing through her that of love. She was well equipped when it came to defending herself, verbally and physically. I may not have been there to witness the 'incident', but she revealed all, and from the rumblings around the area, and remembering what I said of small towns earlier, that day had become etched in folklore. I would have loved to have witnessed it, but it was a bit before my time. Nevertheless, I was in attendance at the court for the proceedings.

In a short time, I experienced the detrimental effect of the weather on air travel, a recently processed crime scene, an execution site and now court proceedings. I am not obliged to enter great detail, but I can reference points.

It all started with Dee being in the right place at the right time, or some may say differently. She foiled an armed robbery attempt, disarming the accused, and sent him through a glass door. The accused, having been apprehended and charged, would press charges against her. Before I go on, I cannot continue without describing the courthouse. The exterior, frozen in time, a piece of history from the 1800s. In the courtyard stood a lone tree, and hanging from the tree, a thermometer. Off in the distant countryside, the sound of a flowing river, only to be heard with a lull in the passing traffic. Anyway, I doubt many are interested in the imagery, so back to the proceedings. The presiding judge asked the plaintiff if he wished to continue, clarifying that he should take a moment to think before answering. The judge added, if he was to proceed and this being a preliminary hearing I think that was the term used. The defendant had the option of the case being heard in-front of a jury and all the details of that ill-fated day would become public knowledge. Further adding, how a petite woman disarmed a man at least twice her weight and size. To me, this was an odd point to mention and yet amusing. I think the judge brought it up knowing that Dee wouldn't face any repercussions for her actions, no matter the outcome, and it would only be a waste of the court's time. However, not knowing of how the system worked in detail, I found the quirkiness of the presiding judge to be interesting, wondering if he was one of a kind or more likely to be encountered in smaller counties and townships.

In the end, there was no further pursuit, with the plaintiff abandoning the case.

Although I omitted quite an amount of details and it might not seem all that interesting to you, the reader, I was glad I could attend; as I was able to see how the system worked as knowing of the exaggerated scenes we see on television and in movies.

As I mentioned, Dee was more than capable of holding her own. It doesn't mean I wouldn't protect or support her.

Our time alone was soon to be short-lived, with an old family friend's arrival. Rick was a veteran and a few times a year; he would have appointments at the Veteran's Hospital.

Instead of having him make long and arduous trips from his home, Dee would have him stay for the duration. She had the room, and that was her nature. Also, it allowed the two of them to catch-up and she could monitor him, in the event he was to undergo a procedure.

I never asked his age. However, based on his service and tours, he was somewhere between his mid-seventies to early eighties.

He was definitely a unique character; never had I met anyone quite like him. Like all of us, he had his quirks, quirks I quickly discovered. His morning routine involved him stirring within his room, making it quite known to all he had awoken. The rooster had some competition! Next, the slow and deliberate shuffle down the hallway with the use of his walking frame, making it known furthermore with the clearing of his throat and a couple of thumps of the walking frame. You might not think much of it, but each aspect unfolded at the same spot, as in the throat clearing and the first thump outside our bedroom door and another thump at the end of the hallway. He would make his way to his preferred armchair, where he would settle himself in. Once comfortable, he released a loud sigh. Within a few seconds of the sigh, the television would spring to life with the volume blaring. Now, if all that had yet to wake you up, he would then yell "Coffee!" As I would come to know Rick, this wasn't coincidental, but rather conceived. Dee was down pat with the routine and I quickly became familiar with it. Let's say we needed to be impeccable with our timing and not waste opportunities when Rick was there, as we did not know if another opportunity may come our way.

Over the years, Dee and I would share a laugh when thinking of Rick and that of his morning routine. It was memories shared and memories no one could steal.

For an older guy with limited mobility, he didn't allow that to stop his curiosity. Something I would quickly learn, particularly when the television fell silent and Rick would yell for one of us to check the cable connections or the satellite dish. We knew he was up and about, especially if we happened to be outside or in the bedroom. Rick had a penchant for having to know all and his mobility was not an issue! During his time with us, we devised and honed many ways to be creative and to communicate. Why you may ask? Let's say it allowed us to briefly slip away if the moment arrived. That communication proved handy many years later when it came to parties and gatherings and not for the reasons implied above.

Having a week to settle in and now a couple of days before his first series of appointments, Dee thought it to be a lovely gesture to make Rick one of his desired dishes...that being chitterlings, sometimes referred to as chitlins and shitlins. If you don't know what they are, you are free to research, but I believe the only true research is experience!

I didn't know what they were, but if I had to go by the names offered, there wasn't much of a desire either. Sometimes things are just better left being mysterious. Rick and others referred to them as a culinary dish of the south. Well, I had my experience and never will I have that experience again. Never! Gumbo, squirrel pie and squirrel stew seemed more culinary! Dee would refer to them as 'the skin of a turd', which was appropriate. Some years later, I would learn of another name, 'Pork Poop Tubes'. Digest that for a moment and envision what they must have looked like, both raw and cooked! If only I could produce a 'scratch and sniff' sticker to share the aroma; you'll never forget! I have come across many smells that I would describe as undesirable, none have come close in comparison to that wretched smell. As the seal of the container broke, the process of diffusion amplified. The smell…the smell blindsided you. That's the best analogy I can provide. However, that wasn't the worst part! Rick liked his cooked in a certain manner and that process just escalated the situation to a biological hazard! The memories and the scent have come flooding back and my stomach is far from impressed! There was no means to combating the smell. The best option, open all the windows and doors and hope for a cross draft to flush the smell. Even then, the smell had a nasty habit of sticking to random items. Believe me, it didn't matter how frigid the air was. To shiver uncontrollably was the only comfortable option. After airing the house for some hours, the smell would dissipate to a 'reasonable' level. When I refer to some hours, I am referring to five or six hours later. Maybe by that time, my sense of smell had become so traumatised, it was no longer an issue. Anyway, Rick enjoyed his 'culinary' delight.

Those wondering, no way in this universe did I even contemplate sampling it! I was fighting hard to keep my stomach from emptying what contents may be inside.

The morning of Rick's first appointments and before the sun rose; we were up and prepping. Dee brewed a fresh pot of coffee to fill Rick's thermos for the trip before brewing a second pot to enjoy before the adventure begun. I grabbed Rick's wheelchair and stowed it in the boot. With overnight temperatures having fallen below freezing, Dee wasn't about to take any chances, allowing Rick to walk down the potentially icy and slippery ramp. He would need to use the mobility elevator, something he loathed. I could imagine he may have thought using the elevator was stripping him of his dignity and independence.

Once on the road, I soon discovered Rick wasn't much of a talker. Maybe it was the trip to the hospital, or maybe it was just his usual self. He wasn't mute throughout, for he would chirp in with a few words here and there, usually asking how much further and how hungry he was. His thermos was quite large; I would estimate it would hold three to four mugs. The trip to the hospital was on average about three-quarters of an hour, and Rick would have that thermos emptied before arriving.

Upon arriving at the Veteran's Hospital, Dee secured a spot not too far from the entrance and near a drainage pit. The drainage pit was probably the most important factor for that day. I would discover more to Rick and his hospital arrival ritual. Dee told me not to be in a hurry to get the wheelchair, just give it a minute or two. I soon discovered why, as it coincided with the drainage pit! Rick would open his door and emptied what few drops of coffee may have remained in his thermos onto the bitumen and into the pit. However, it didn't stop there! Oh, no! Rick then opened the valve of his catheter bag, emptying his bodily waste. Dee would argue, as she did that day, but he refused to empty it appropriately, like the hospital restroom, because of his pride. I could understand and still do today, but there is always a solution to a problem and a better solution to the one in-place.

It took some creativity to set up the chair and get Rick into it without either of us coming in contact with the bio-hazard.

The walk wasn't all that far, and considering it was a warm day; quite pleasurable. Rounding the corner, the entrance of the hospital. Immediately, I recognised it from the pictures Dee had shared over the years. The courtyard, trees strategically placed for shade in the warmer months and, of course, the ground to sky glass of the entrance, reflecting not only the massive flag flowing, but the blue sky and the drifting clouds. Words just don't seem adequate to describe the reflection. It is something that you need see to truly comprehend and appreciate.

Although the outside didn't resemble that of a hospital, there was no mistaking it was a hospital once entering; the smell and appearance of sterility and the uneasy feeling arising. Dee and Rick were on a first name basis with majority of the staff. Typical me, I lingered just behind, trying to remain as inconspicuous as one could. Once you've had ample experience, you'd be surprised how easy it does become to blend into the background. It was challenging as it was a Veteran's Hospital and not your standard run-of-the-mill hospital. After a few impromptu stops for a quick meet and greet, Dee guided Rick into what I would describe as a common room. Rick took control, wheeling himself further into the room to position himself at one of the few tables with his friends. Just through my observations, he was very particular about who and where he actually positioned himself at the table.

The room loud with chatter, laughter, and arguments. Dee and I remained near the door, but in the corridor, chatting amongst ourselves while watching the antics of the room. If I was to describe the atmosphere, I would say…high school. There were groups, and within those groups, some were closer than others. Just like high school, you had those on the outer, intentionally excluded from any activity or interaction.

Society does not change!

Watching Rick interact, Dee and I couldn't do anything but laugh. It was unmistakable, who was and wasn't his friend. There was one moment where he was enjoying a conversation with another table across the room without missing a beat and yet, when someone seated just across from him, who he wasn't friends tried to ask him a couple of questions, Rick suddenly became hard of hearing!

It still makes me laugh to this day.

This January day would prove to be a significant moment for me, as I would have two unexpected interactions, both impacting my life and one that continues to resonate with me today.

Dee popped her head into the room to let Rick know it was time for his first appointment. Amazingly, he didn't have any trouble hearing her. Yes, I am having a tiny dig there, but in good spirits! Rick pushed himself away from the table before navigating his way out. Once in the corridor, Dee took control of the grips and we headed down the corridors to his first appointment. We stopped outside a nurse's station, where a couple of nurses started chatting with their favourite patient. It was wonderful to see the human interaction; these veterans were people and not just a name on a folder or an identification number. I overheard them asking who I was and without hesitation and at the top of his voice; he told them I was his friend who came all the way from Australia. It was touching, and it honoured me to see how proud and excited he was. However, I was trying to remain as inconspicuous as possible, and I had achieved that, until that precise moment.

With Rick and Dee disappearing into a room at the end of the corridor, a young veteran (I would say he was in his late twenties) came rolling up to me, where he didn't even question if I was the right person, he just came out and told me I was the Australian guy he heard about and I needed to say something; he wanted to hear my accent. I just smiled and quietly said hey! But he wouldn't leave it. He continued to ask me to say something. At the best of times, I speak little, often referred to as a man of few words. To make both of us feel content, I asked which branch did he serve, but he never did answer. In all his excitement, he continued to ask if I would say more. A nurse soon appeared; informing him the doctor was ready and wheeled him away. As he was wheeled down the corridor, he yelled he would be back.

In retrospect, I'm glad he was excited. I didn't know about his life. He might have experienced a terrible day, and with me just saying a few words, may have brightened his day. I believe he was there to receive an upgrade to an electric wheelchair.

The hospital housed many veterans on a long-term basis. For some, this place would be their last home. I discovered many either had no family or no family close-by. Other than the interaction from the regulars of the hospital; occasionally receiving a visit from a friend, but ultimately, were quite willing to interact with anyone willing to take the time to listen. I recall the immense sadness I felt entering the hospital and learning of their stories.

Dee and Rick re-emerged, rolling down the corridor. Rick seemed to be in higher spirits. With some time before his next appointment, we headed down to the cafeteria to grab some lunch. As we set off, my new friend was in his electric wheelchair and having some difficulties with the steering. As we waited for the elevator, he was becoming more and more frustrated with his inability to steer and navigate a relatively easy turn. I wanted to help, but Dee told me he needed to learn and find success for himself. It may sound harsh, but actually, it is compassionate. They were once independent people who suffered a disease or an injury that left them feeling as if they had their independence stripped. Every frustration leads to success and builds confidence in their independence.

Dee decided not to take the direct route to the cafeteria from the elevator. Instead, taking the scenic route that left Rick far from impressed and by the sounds emanating from his stomach, it too! I'm sure there was something living inside him. The scenic route took us past the main entrance once again. Something within drew my attention outside and to the sky. Whatever was drawing me, I am glad I didn't resist. I have always had a passion for weather and the sky. I was far from familiar with the weather patterns of the US, but ominous is ominous and instinct is instinct. Having pointed out the distant sky to Dee, with confidence, she told me they weren't snow producing clouds and thunderstorms were a rarity for the time of year. She was familiar, and I had confidence in her; therefore, I pushed any thoughts to the back of my mind.

Apparently, the cafeteria was the place to be. It was verging on capacity. Rick was elated, ordering a banquet for himself! Dee and I shared a bowl of wedges. Rick downed his banquet, leaving no evidence! Now, that wasn't the amazing part either. What happened next took me by surprise, as Rick wasn't the only person in that cafeteria to do this. He grabbed a few serviettes and spread them on the table in-front of him.

He then took a sip of his water, swirling it around his mouth, before spitting the contents of into an empty cup. What followed was the eye opener! He removed his dentures, held them over the 'waste' cup and poured his water, rinsing said dentures. Then, he made sure not to use all his water, saving some, placing his dentures onto the serviettes and with another serviette, patted dry his dentures. Once dry, or at least sufficiently, he re-seated them before drinking the rest of his water. As I sat there bewildered, I looked across to Dee and she was merely shaking her head, as this was usual practice. By the time we prepared to leave the cafeteria, I caught sight of another person performing something very similar to Rick.

Some things should never be seen.

Rick's last appointment of the day was a minor procedure, and he was quite entitled to his lunch, as it bore no impact. By the time the procedure took place, it was mid-afternoon, and the hospital was becoming quieter, as visitors were now departing. Let's just say that the corridors echoed much more than usual and we were left in tears of laughter as we sat waiting for Rick. The more we tried to contain our laughter, the more it flowed! It had been a long time since I laughed so hard and had someone to share in the laughter.

Having his procedure successfully completed and denying, he uttered a single word during the entire procedure; although, evidence and witnesses dispute his account, Rick wanted to stop by the common room to say goodbye. This, the moment where I would meet Charlie. Dee had mentioned Charlie in our many conversations and hoped we would meet. Rick nonchalantly wheeled himself into the room and positioned himself once more at the same table as earlier that day. As we observed, still with the odd chuckle, Charlie came rolling from the corridor behind. When I mention rolling, I don't mean in the term of a wheelchair. Charlie was confined to a modified stretcher. At the rear, two smaller wheels similar to a wheelchair's front wheels; for steering and up front, two considerably larger wheels designed for propulsion. Charlie could turn that stretcher on a five-cent piece if need be.

Listening to Dee and Charlie speak, you could hear the respect and admiration they shared and the friendship that was bonding. Having introduced us, Charlie and I would end up in a deep discussion. I discovered he served multiple tours in Vietnam. It was there where he suffered his injuries. He was quite open and willing to share of his experiences, not holding anything back, blowing my mind with specific and graphical details. And yet, here he was, always carrying a smile and a positive attitude to match. I cannot even imagine what might dwell inside him, but what I know is that even on his bad days, he still put on that smile and uplifted everyone around. Truly a unique and amazing guy!

Chatting with Charlie, I understood his driving force. Life doesn't always provide equality and fairness. It can be downright unfair as it can be horrific, and he wanted people to see and understand that point. He also wanted people to know of the enjoyments and blessings life can bring. It was important to live life as each day arose and to spend it with someone you love. Relying on friends and family is nice, but it's not the same as having that special someone.

Those words resonated with the younger version of myself and have much more of a meaning to me today.

I gained a better understanding of the hell the troops endured on the lines, within the confines of camp and their return home. What sticks out is Charlie's description of men in war. There being three types, those who will become gripped with fear, unable to return fire when fired upon. The second, being of those who will fire when fired upon and the last being of those who have no issue with pulling the trigger, no matter enemy or friend. He would continue to mention how war changes a person. Whether mentally or physically, everyone returns changed. Some return broken. The rigours experienced in war do not discriminate. Many were unwilling participants, forced into action, fighting against their beliefs and for a cause unbeknownst to them. Returning home, the people abused them and, in time, forgotten, but to become a footnote in history.

Having spent that time with Charlie and Rick, I always had this desire to write a poem inspired from my encounter and their shared memories. If you had yet to guess, I enjoy the written word and have a tendency to lean towards poetry to express myself. However, I would continue to hold off from writing anything, as I felt it would not only stir emotions, emotions they may have buried for whatever the reason may be, but I wouldn't be able to write a piece that would preserve their memories. If I am being honest, I felt any attempt would be a form of an insult if I could not get it right. They both have long since passed away. Some years later, I would eventually pen the piece 'Sullen'. I would categorise it as one of the better pieces I've penned, that coming from my harshest critic, me. I have a great distaste for reading my works once written, as I have a tendency to edit them. However, with Sullen, I find it difficult to read because of the raw emotion and memories it stirs. I am confident that both men would have given their blessings. It is unfortunate that it took me years to find the courage and belief within myself. That doubt denied Charlie and Rick the opportunity to read the poem, they were the inspiration behind.

We would eventually leave the hospital an hour or two later. Walking into the courtyard, my eyes once again drawn to the ominous sky. The definition…the intensity and the menace, the colour and contrast just worked well to emphasise the ominous feel. It appeared to my naked eye; the system was heading in our direction and moving rather quickly. I brought the ominous skyline to Dee's attention again. She took a suitable moment to look and agreed it looked ominous, but thought we might be in for a drenching.

On the road and just beginning the journey home, Rick made it known to all of his hunger. With it just past five and the traffic, it might be another forty-five to sixty minutes of drive time. Dee agreed to stop somewhere so he could get something to hold him over. I was sure he would be hungry by the time we arrived home, no matter how much he ate. As we continued, the weather system continued encroaching and the light slowly fading by the sheer influence of the ominous clouds. We pulled into Taco Bell and started towards the drive-thru, Rick made it clear he wanted to eat inside. So, Dee drove past the drive-thru and into the car park. As she shifted the car into park, a significant gust of wind hit the car, shaking it noticeably! She tried to have Rick reconsider the drive-thru, but he would have nothing of it! So, Dee changed tactics. She told Rick that if he could make it to the front door, then we would eat in. The wind had since whipped up; loose trash swirling. Rick's look towards Dee was that best described as defiance. As he opened the door, a gust of wind slammed the door shut. Don't worry, Rick was okay, free of injury. He tried once more to open the door, but with the wind truly gusting, he was no match. Large drops of rain thudded on the car and Dee quickly put the car in gear and drove around to the drive-thru window, where, by a stroke of fortune, was free of cars. The thuds of rain quickly transformed into golf ball sized hail! The building to the left, the roof over-hang and the fence and shrubs to the right provided some protection.

What happened next, I shall never forget…a dream come true!

The wind tore through, juddering the car as if it weighed nothing! The shrubs, parallel to the ground. The sound of the wind and hail…deafening. The best I can describe it, as you are reading this…that of the voice inside your head that comes to life when reading. Well, you wouldn't have been able to hear that voice! As I looked out the rear window, I witnessed the moment two industrial garbage bins became airborne and something else quickly zoomed by. Whatever it was, it was substantial.

I was living a dream! Not only did I see a tornado with my eyes, I experienced the tornado as it passed over the car! What appeared as an eternity lasted only a minute or two at most. Once safe, we drove out to examine the damage. Debris littered the landscape! Roofs torn from their buildings and scattered in neighbouring businesses, power lines down, trees damaged, windows shattered and so much more. Apart from the destruction generated, I thought the moment to be amazing! To see, hear and feel the brute power and wrath of nature and survive…wow!

We would navigate the debris to make our way home. The damage to the area was significant. Later that night, we would see the images of the destruction plastered across the television. Seeing it on television just doesn't capture the sheer force of nature.

The memory will forever remain with me, and it was the only day I didn't have the camcorder!

Rick had lost his appetite by the time we arrived home. Actually, if it wasn't for Rick's appetite, we would have been on the road, driving into the teeth of the tornado with no protection. Although an amazing experience; truly a sobering moment. Life can be ripped from us and by any means.

I would like to believe there was an intervention that afternoon. Yes, we could have survived out on the road; our odds of survival were favourable in the drive-thru of the Taco Bell.

The following morning is when we learnt of the details surrounding the tornado. No lives lost, a handful of people suffered minor injuries, the damage bill was considerable and the bureau preliminarily rated the tornado as an EF3, later downgraded to an EF2. What made the entire event eerie was that the official start to the tornado season was still a few months away.

Some of you are probably wondering if I would experience a tornado again! I can confidently say yes! Being older now and considering other factors, I would not place myself in the firing line. I would have a still camera and film rolling from a safe distance though.

Rick's last appointment would fall four days after the tornado. Driving through the area, if you weren't aware of the event, then you wouldn't know. Some damage was still clear, but nothing that would jump out, screaming tornado! Credit where credit is due. The team of workers responsible for clean-up and repair did not only one hell of a job, but an amazing job!

The hospital was much quieter. Dee once again left me to my own devices as she escorted Rick to his appointment. I found myself in an eerily quiet common room. There wasn't a soul, and it didn't look as if anyone had been there. An upright piano stood in the far corner and I had to check it out. Being close to it, I could see the weathered look and still some of the finer details of the design. The history the piano absorbed was something I could only imagine. I know a few people who would look upon the piano and either have the piano restored to a pristine condition or throw it away. I would leave the piano in its current state. It brings character and life. That's my opinion. I hit a few keys and even I could tell the piano was in need of tuning. While I was there, I wasn't worried about it not being in tune. The only song I could remember was the one I started playing. You are likely wondering the song! Well, that will remain a secret. I was so enthralled in the moment; I hadn't noticed Dee and Charlie lingering around the door. Once I heard her voice, I quickly stopped playing. If I play, I play for my enjoyment and privately. Anyway, this would be the last time I would see and talk with Charlie. Meeting him was definitely a moment of the trip and a life-changing experience. Our brief encounter not only provided a lasting impact, it provided an opportunity to meet this wonderful and inspiring man, who I called my friend.

Charlie was battling cancer, and he was losing his battle. He never let it be known, so it came as quite a shock when I found out a few months after returning to Australia he had passed away. Charlie may have been an older guy, but he was young at heart! He had his experiences and life might not have turned out the way he may have wanted, but in his presence, he brought light and lifted the atmosphere.

The way life unfolds, it doesn't always make sense.

As for Rick, he would return home later that week. We remained in contact until his passing.

Being alone once more, Dee suggested we take a road trip. The options were…north to New Jersey or south to North Carolina. At both locations, we would spend a weekend with her friends. The decision was to head south and to North Carolina, where I would have the opportunity to see the historical locations of Kitty Hawk, where the Wright brothers made their first successful flight, visit Cape Hatteras Light, a renowned lighthouse and to discover more of the lost colony of Roanoke.

Of course, I knew of the history surrounding New Jersey, but little did I know the history. If I knew what I would learn years later when we somehow talked about that road trip, I would definitely have pushed for New Jersey.

Chapter 6

In retrospect, rather than use the word trip, I probably should use adventure, possibly even calamity.

The morning of, I would learn that our road trip would also include a passenger. To say it blindsided me would be an understatement. Our passenger would be a friend of Dee's, Alice. While in North Carolina, we would spend a couple of nights with another of Dee's friends, Sally, who also was the partner of Alice. Alice had been visiting relatives in the state and after discovering of Dee's intention; she saved some money on an airfare and hitched a ride. Of course, it was disappointing we wouldn't be on the road alone, but it provided an opportunity to discover more of Dee's world.

Alice had the advantage, knowing more of me than I of her. However, she would never refer to me by name, always opting to refer to me as BK. Alice was free-spirited and enjoyed her special beverage. Her referring to me as BK didn't bother me, it only puzzled me! Curiosity had me wondering the reason behind BK, but I also enjoy a challenge and being a road trip, it could provide some entertainment. Before considering the possibility of probing Alice's mind, I was running everything I could through my mind that may relate to or explain BK. I had come up with nothing! There had to be some resemblance of logic behind it.

Crossing into North Carolina, our journey would take us across a bridge. Unfortunately, the name of the bridge eludes me, but I remember Alice insisting the bridge was eight miles long! I wasn't familiar with the area, but I had my doubts over her claims, mainly because of the amount of beverages she had consumed up to this point and that I could see the end of the bridge in the not too far distance. I will say she was partially right in her statement, with the miles, just not the eight. Having just entered onto the bridge, I leaned over to take a peek at the odometer and noted the starting value. Alice from the backseat explicitly told me the hundreds of times she had ventured across this bridge. Typical me, I gave her many opportunities to retract her claim, but she rightly informed me I use that weird system of measurement and wouldn't have an idea. Well, little did she know I was familiar with both units. Upon exiting the bridge, I peeked again at the odometer and I can say with confidence it wasn't even close to the eight miles. As they say, it wasn't even in the ballpark. In the spirit of kindness, I won't reveal the actual distance. Yet, I was wrong, according to Alice. I was not American, so I didn't understand how to read the numbers. Playful banter ensued for a while until we reached a service station. As Alice disappeared into the restrooms, I took the moment to ask if Alice had always been this way. Dee explained how her transformation took place. That is why it is important to never judge a person, period. We leave our imprint in the sand that no other can match.

Before starting the last leg, and with Alice still disposed of, I filled Dee in with my plan to have some fun with her

(Alice). Typical Australian humour and the odd yarn. Hey, it's every Australian's duty to joke around in a respectful, but outlandish manner.

As Alice found her way to the car, Dee without hesitation asked her what BK stood for! She was as confused and curious as I. Alice simply replied, British King. Dee and I looked at each, somewhat puzzled, before breaking into laughter. It took a moment to calm ourselves and suck in the oxygen, when we did, Dee quipped, "You know he is Australian and not British?" Bless her heart, without missing a beat, Alice's reply, "there's no difference…they're the same." Like I said, bless her heart. However, what I learnt that day was to never allow Alice to navigate. She didn't know distance and apparently geography was not a strong feature as well.

Knowing Alice's knowledge of Australia was extremely limited, it was time to spin a couple of yarns. And so it begun with the mere mention of how in remote areas of Australia, some children travelling to and from school would use kangaroos, because of their abundant nature and our vision of a greener future. There was doubt in her eyes for a moment, but Dee chipped in convincing her with the claim; having mentioned a documentary she recently watched and an article she read some months earlier, which included photos. She referenced how the kids used the big red kangaroos and not the smaller grey kangaroos. In addition, I mentioned of the kangaroo's intellect level and those outside of Australia would be unaware of how intelligent the species is. Fortunately, back in the 1960s, a documentary was made on the life of a kangaroo named Skippy. I suggested that she search for Skippy on the Internet. Even in the Internet's infancy, there were AVI files of Skippy, minus the audio. Dee and I must have been convincing enough and her judgement impaired, as she believed what we had fed her and admired how progressive but strange Australia was.

I could have ended it there, but I was interested in how far I could push the limits of believability! Next, the crocodile!

The crocodile, influenced by comments made by Alice earlier and how Australian men seemed relaxed, well defined and fit. So, I explained we needed ourselves to be in order to not only protect our significant other and family, but ourselves. The gym wasn't all that necessary, unless you lived in either the cities or suburbs. For those living in specific regions in the north of Australia, most workouts came in the morning and evening through wrestling of crocodiles. Stepping outside provided its challenges. One would need to remain relaxed, but alert, for a crocodile was usually lurking and ready to attack. Crocodiles were more adventurous and aggressive during those periods. Therefore, wrestling encounters were quite common. It was perfect mostly. The act of wrestling helped to build strength and endurance. It also provided a valuable lesson regarding thinking in the heat of battle and how not to lose focus for even a millisecond. The look on her face was priceless! I can see it now! Selling the scenario further, I may have mentioned that the crocodiles sometimes win, particularly when a person is weak or loses focus. That's the cycle of life. Those strong enough will survive, and will survive to reproduce. Alice's reaction was, as expected...shoot 'em all. As I then explained, they are a protected species, so just the mere act of attempting to shoot one, would land you in gaol.

Alice made it crystal clear...there was no way she could live there, nor would she visit. Australia was wild, crazy, and untamed.

Of course, how could I not finish with the infamous Drop Bear? I was sure that would push her over the 'freaking out' edge, but just to make sure...I thought I may also need to mention the magpie. A crazy bird that enjoys preying on unsuspecting people, swooping from heights at speed to pluck out eyes and if not eyes, then some brain matter. From there, I couldn't resist...I had to mention the creatures in the water and on the land that could injure you or, worse, kill you. Basically, everything in Australia was either dangerous or deadly. The colour in Alice's face drained. She made it very clear that anyone living in Australia was insane!

I'm sure in time, she realised we were having but some fun.

Arriving at Sally's, pulling into the drive, it was different. In the middle stood a modified trailer, the exterior tastefully renovated and the properties borderline surrounded by trees. If you're not familiar with trailers, they were and probably still are a cost-effective means to owning a home. I've seen some amazing trailers you wouldn't be aware were trailers; the exterior and interior renovations, amazing! The downside, one could say a tornado seemed drawn to them. That is pure speculation though.

A small landing perched slightly above the ground stood in-front of the entrance. Waiting was Sally. As Alice exited the car, she adamantly explained to Sally they were never to visit Australia! Sally, bewildered and understandably so. Anyhow, Sally welcomed us and into her home, pointing us to the room where we could drop off our bags and invited us to wander and explore the property.

An opportunity to explore was also an opportunity for alone time. The house itself was quite spacious and well kept. However, the bathroom was of concern and not for the reasons you may be thinking. The bathroom compared to the other rooms was tiny! The ceiling was much lower than the other ceilings in the house. Without being accurate, I stand over six feet (one hundred and eighty plus centimetres). When standing in the shower/tub combo, my head pressed against the ceiling. The height of the shower rose; mid-chest level. I had the option of hunching over or squatting. I would like to know who the mastermind behind this one room was! How do you manage such a spacious layout for the rest of the living quarters, but destroy the bathroom, one of the most important rooms!

Continuing our exploration, we discovered more. First, we met Sally's two cats, one of which will play a significant role later. I'm a dog lover, and I think cats know this, particularly this one. As we moved along, we came across what appeared to be a new extension, but oddly, it was not in use. From the doorway looking in, it became clear why the room was not in use. To say the floor was uneven would not only be an understatement, it would be misleading. A splash of paint and some contrast, the theory of gravity could be well explained. Add another analogy; the roughest of oceans could not match the waves of this floor! To me, this was perplexing and intriguing. Let's just say I am much wiser in my older age. I couldn't help myself and I had to walk into the room. I made sure Dee remained outside, not only for her safety, but if I needed someone to call for help! Two weight-transferring steps were enough for me to reconsider what the hell I had just done! I'm not sure if I can describe the experience with justice, but I will try. The sensation was one of uneasiness. There was a sway that I would best describe as jelly, jelly not completely set, the outside firm, but still liquid within. Thankfully, I do not suffer from motion sickness, as I'm sure the room would have triggered it. I didn't spend any longer than necessary in there, slowly re-tracing my steps and making sure not to unnecessarily shift my weight, fearing I could bring the room crashing down. Having finally made my way to 'firm' ground, Dee mentioned that with the slightest of movements I made, the room moved, not just the floor! Seriously, a wayward sneeze could have this extension demolished.

Skipping ahead and into the evening, we sat down in the living room, chatting, sharing stories, some sad, some embarrassing and some hilarious. It was a relaxing and enjoyable moment. Everyone was having a good time. With the night growing longer, we all decided to retire for the evening; as we headed towards our respective rooms. On approaching our room, there was a distinct odour wafting, the unmistakable fragrance of cat defecation, or at least to my nose. Upon entering the room, the pungent odour became unbearable. *(However, more bearable than chitterlings.)* Powering on the lights with the flick of the switch, the room illuminated and, to our horror, before us, dead centre of the bed was a massive pile of cat defecation! Just mentioning the incident conjures vivid memories. I turned to Dee and just by the look on her face, there was no amount of cleaning that would see us touch that bed! We have boundaries and that is one! Dee was in disbelief at the surprise left for us.

We would end up spending the night on the couch. The couch may have been comfortable to sit on, but for sleeping...it was horrendous! The slope made for a sleepless night. We would rate this experience as our worst night of sleep either of us had ever experienced.

Come the much anticipated morning, we rose to freshen up before sharing in breakfast with Sally and Alice. It was at breakfast; Dee could not refrain any longer, revealing the events of the night and our decision to cut our stay short. Sally, shocked and disappointed, but Alice, she struggled to hold back the laughter.

After breakfast, we gathered our bags, thanked Sally and Alice for their hospitality and the opportunity to visit. We jumped in the car and spent the day sightseeing. In particular, Dee was keen to show me Hatteras and Roanoke Island. Both places were exciting for me to visit; the opportunity to explore the islands and learn more of the Lost Colony of Roanoke. I'd heard of the first colony before meeting her, but it was she who brought it to life and piqued my curiosity. How does a colony simply vanish? I have my theories of what may have happened to the colony and Hatteras seems logical and yet, not convincing in my opinion. I don't think we'll ever know, just another mystery in the chapter of humanity. Next on the agenda was that of the lighthouse, Cape Hatteras Light. Because of mitigation efforts to help prevent further erosion, the lighthouse was closed to the public, but even from a distance, its presence was remarkable and something to be admired. It was disappointing not to get closer or enter the lighthouse, but what is, is!

Time to head home and before leaving North Carolina behind us, a stop at Kitty Hawk was required. Like Hatteras, it too was closed, but I still stood on the ground where Wilbur and Orville stood on the day of their successful flight. It was a grounding moment. I would have loved to have seen more, but it wasn't meant to be.

With North Carolina in the rear-view mirror, it wasn't too long before we intersected a small storm cell that produced hail between the sizes of a pea and a golf ball. Again, an unusual occurrence for the time of the year, but I wasn't complaining. Dee found a few small trees which offered some protection to the car. As we waited for the conditions to at least ease, we turned up the radio and just enjoyed the moment.

Chapter 7

By now, we had settled into life, living as a couple.

Over the course of the following month, we delved deeper into the tragedies of Dee's life. She held nothing back, including the tears and the raw emotions. I knew some details, but to hear her walkthrough each moment was heart-wrenching. Not only did it take time for me to process, it shook me to my very core. I made a promise to her and I have no intention of breaking that promise. What she revealed will never leave these lips! What she had to and continued to endure was testament to not only her character, but to her strength, determination, and love.

I was ready to stay and build a future together, but I couldn't ignore nor disregard the memories and pain that dwelt within her. We sat down to discuss at length our future, finally arriving at the consensus that Australia would be the better place to start our life and from there, the secret property search ensued. Dee used her connections, both locally and abroad, as well as utilising the Internet to research general information and statistics of areas. Real estate sites didn't exist or, if there were any, they were known to very few. We narrowed down our search to the Margaret River region of Western Australia. The information received was promising, with pricing being reasonable and within our budget. That isn't a term I thought I'd use in a sentence when referring to real estate...'pricing being reasonable'.

It wasn't long into the search when Dee surprised me with the news...we were to be parents! Both of us overjoyed and terrified. The odds of her conceiving were ridiculous. When I say ridiculous, I truly mean out of this world! Her odds of being struck by lightning twice in her lifetime and that of winning the jackpot lottery as a solo winner were far more realistic, and that is no exaggeration. When younger, she suffered an accident, which left her with severe and irreversible injuries. It was truly a miracle she survived and a miracle to have conceived.

Unbelievable! We were going to parents! Never had the idea of being a father crossed my mind and here I was, excited and yet petrified. I knew Dee would make a wonderful mother, absolutely no doubt. Finding a property now became much more urgent.

Our last night together, State side of course. We enjoyed a lovely dinner at a local restaurant. Anyone unfamiliar with the area would never know such an establishment existed. Tucked away inconspicuously within the city limits of a small town. Amongst the residential homes, a few businesses stood.

There was no roadside signage, although, I believe that has since changed, and yet, the place was a hit, always packed to capacity. The atmosphere was electric and the food, amazing! Southern cuisine being the specialty, but it also had a unique twist. There was no skimping on servings! No matter the dish or course, they guaranteed you'd receive a feed that was worth every penny and more. I'll admit that it disappointed me we hadn't made it there sooner. Coming from a person who avoids large gatherings, it speaks volumes not only for the food on offer, but of the family-owned business.

Of course, my curiosity got the better of me, and I had to see what I could find online about the establishment. The restaurant has since undergone significant renovations inside and out. I'm disappointed with the exterior renovation. The inconspicuous look added character and an air of mystery, especially when arriving and doubting there was a restaurant until you walked in. Of course, the menu needs to change with the times, but I hope it still features some dishes from all those years ago. If I do return, I will stop in.

The morning was sombre, not at all unexpected. We had started our life together and were blessed with a magical moment. Even with all the mishaps along the way, it couldn't detract. Plus, those mishaps became memories and without those memories, the beginning of this memoir would be lacking. I wouldn't change one moment. Each was and is important; playing a defining role in our relationship, future memories, and laughs. All that led me to where I am today.

The air was crisp, the sky cloudless and blue. I was just tying up a few loose ends with my packing; strategically leaving behind a pair of jeans and a shirt. I knew Dee would eventually discover them, just a small reminder of me, even though she was to fly out a week or two later, having to remain behind to tie up some loose ends. Come to think of it, there's a lot of tying of loose ends! We grew during our time together, and this time apart was going to be difficult. The thought was playing on my mind; I walked around one last time, to clear my thoughts and to admire the scenery and the history. You never know if you'll return to a place. Cherish the moment and create the memories. Looking out across to the neighbouring property, between two dilapidated tobacco sheds were the rusted shells of two cars. Because of the wooded over-growth, it was impossible to determine the make or model. Without seeing the shells up close, there was a fifty-fifty shot of either of them being of value. Soon I rejoined reality, stowing my bags into the car and leaving the property I had come to call home for one last time.

The airport run was uneventful and 'long'. Music was playing and neither one of us saying much. Our emotions were running on high. Dee focused on the road and I would alternate between watching her and the scenery.

Remember how I mentioned emotions were high? That was clear at the airport. I didn't expect it would be as tough as it was. We had fallen in love and that love grew to deepen over the time we shared in each other's lives. I'm neither ashamed nor embarrassed to admit I had tears welling in my eyes, and that welling turned to flowing saltwater during our last hug. She didn't want to let me go, as I didn't want to let her go, but I had to. I was aware how it was eating me up inside, and I only could imagine how she was feeling. As I turned around and checked myself in, I couldn't help to wonder if I was making the right decision. Should I be leaving now? Should I be leaving her when pregnant? If I had additional time, I likely would have left the terminal and remained, only to work out the details and complications later. It's now history. I boarded the flight and headed for O'Hare.

On approach to O'Hare, with the sun setting, Lake Michigan shimmered and standing proud from the surrounding scenery, the John Hancock Centre. As the plane landed, I thought how great it was not to be thrown around like a rag doll. Don't let that fool you! The trip home wasn't without adventure, but there was no comparison!

I had approximately an hour and a half to locate my next gate. It seemed like ample time; although I was sceptical, I was still upbeat! What I was unaware before landing was of the renovations undertaken. It became quite challenging when signage was removed or covered. But I wasn't worried; I had survived more challenging situations. As I meandered around the terminal, in search of the gate, I noticed I wasn't the only one turned about. I like to challenge myself and find my own conclusions, so I am reluctant, at least early on, to burden another for help. *I completed a circuit of either the terminal or a section of terminal, at least, I think,* returning to the gate where it all started. One good point: I wasn't lost. I knew exactly where I was. It was reminiscent of my first trip to Canberra, where I ended at the point I started. I knew they would announce the boarding of the flight over the PA system, so I just needed to remain patient, wait and watch. In retrospect, it all could have gone pear shaped if the PA system was taken offline or it was a silent airport, such as Dubai today. Anyway, the call bellowed out, and I made the short walk to the gate, where airline staff removed the covers over the various signs.

Remember, I did tip you off regarding issues and what nots. The electronic boarding system conveniently was down. Staff and techs frantically worked to restore the system, but were unsuccessful in their attempts. Hence, boarding became a manual process, slowing the process, thus delaying departure by twenty minutes.

Seriously, you thought the return leg was to be without incident? You are truly optimistic.

The flight into LAX was smooth, and as a bonus, the cabin was quite empty. I had some space to stretch out my legs. To this day, the only flight I have flown that hasn't been at capacity and left feeling like a sardine.

The flight touched down at LAX in the late evening. Knowing of the delay, the heart rate was slightly elevated, for it could be touch and go to make the last leg.

However, there were five of us in need of making that connection to Australia, and five of us sprinting with carry-on luggage in tow, from one end of the terminal to the opposite end. We all made the gate in time; some of us may have lost a lung somewhere along the way.

The trip home was uneventful, except for losing an entire day. I guess it was only fair, seeing as I experienced the longest Boxing Day. My mind on that trip home, occupied with thoughts of Dee, the pregnancy and how I should have turned around at the gate and remained with her.

Little would I realise, some years further into my journey, how life can imitate itself.

Chapter 8

Having touched down in Sydney in the early hours of the morning, I allowed myself a day to reconfigure my biological settings.

For reasons unbeknownst to me, I was unable to reach Dee. I made many attempts, all concluding with the same result. I used everything available from ICQ and PowWow to email and the phone. It wasn't out of character, so I wasn't overly concerned. It made me reconsider my decision to not remain with her, though. In the meantime, I tried to distract myself constructively, continuing to research potential property options. I will say it wasn't much of a distraction, as my thoughts continued to circle back to Dee.

She would call later that night; I was quite relieved to hear her voice, but my intuition was telling me something was amiss, so I asked. What she would say in response would inevitably change our lives forever.

Dee would explain how she had an ultrasound appointment. By my rough estimations, and I mean rough, I was somewhere high above the blue waters of the Pacific Ocean. However, it didn't explain her absence. There was a lengthy pause before her now shaky voice re-emerged. She suffered a miscarriage. It left me speechless. We knew there was always a significant chance considering her injuries, but you tend not to focus on the negatives, especially as days numbered without incident. You look for positives and focus on them. Dee's odds of carrying to term were barely stronger than her odds of conceiving. That was our reality. There was an air of optimism from the moment she conceived and each day without incident. The world fell silent after hearing of the miscarriage. Life stopped as everything we knew was not only flipped inside and out, it had been obliterated! Never should I have left her behind. I should have remained with her. Why didn't I trust my intuition?

To say it was devastating would only serve as an injustice. The word devastation cannot express the vivid and treacherous emotions raging within. It overcame me with the sensation of coldness as not only my body, but my soul fell numb. My appetite became non-existent and the only pain I could feel through the numbness was that of my heart breaking.

Here we were, stranded on opposite sides of the Pacific Ocean…needing each other. We should've been comforting each other. I not only felt helpless, I felt worthless. What I was experiencing was incomparable to that of Dee. Not only did I have my emotions, I was absorbing hers. Overwhelming and excruciating.

Regrettably, I would come to endure such emotions some years later.

Overcome with guilt, I would question my decision for years to come.

During the call, Dee explained the D & C procedure she was scheduled to undertake, otherwise known as dilation and curettage. Our closeness allowed us to anticipate one another's actions and thoughts. However, I didn't see this one. I wanted to be on the next available flight, however, she insisted not to waste the money. She would fly out a week later than scheduled. We argued over me flying out before coming to an agreement. She then explained what she had planned and where she decided to lay our child to rest.

Dee would email two pictures of the final resting place. Fourteen pink flowers adorned the earth.

Never did we think we would be parents, let alone conceive we would bury our child. The world ceased to exist in my view. Nothing mattered! As no one knew of the pregnancy, we kept this pain to ourselves. Within, I was dying. No parent…no parent should have to say goodbye and bury their child. Why? I still search for the answer to this, knowing I will never find what I am looking for. With each passing day, I ended up neglecting parts of my life. One consequence was losing the opportunity to secure a property. However, my love for Dee and her love for me never wavered.

Life is anything but smooth sailing.

When Dee finally arrived, we isolated ourselves from the world, just holding and comforting each other. The silence, deafening and the tears flowed. Holding her, I could feel her immeasurable pain. I would have taken it all. We expressed everything that needed to be expressed through our tears and embrace.

Over the course of the next few days, I would put pen to paper. I needed a constructive outlet to express my raw emotions and to say sorry. It took everything within me to pen the words. To read those words, I just couldn't. I handed what I had penned to Dee. She would end up in tears and once composing herself; she handed me what she had written. Her words allowed me to feel and share in her pain and anguish. Her words illustrated our child's final resting place, the weather of the day, the sounds echoing and her beautiful words spoken, as she said goodbye.

All these years later, here I am writing and I still find it difficult.

From our expressions, I would later work to have the two pieces come together. Having done so, I wouldn't look upon the piece until the unfolding of future events.

I am aware we all have different processes and thoughts. After all, we are individuals. Some may feel my locking away of memories and emotions as my attempt to forget the pain. You would be correct to a point. Rather, I was trying to numb the pain. There hasn't been a day over the years I haven't thought about our child. Envisioning of their firsts…steps, words, birthday and school and a variety of other situations, including the terrible twos, dating and my reaction. I could go on. I am thankful they didn't have to see what the future held.

I only started speaking openly of my child when future events unfolded, as you'll soon discover. During those events, I learnt Dee had shared the loss with my mum, some years later. She saw Mum as her mum and not an in-law, as Mum saw Dee as another daughter. I can only imagine the number of times that I was the focal point of their conversations. Yes, I can frustrate people. Most introverts do! Needless to say, I loved them both deeply.

It is amazing what you learn. Dee would fall pregnant a few years after the heartache. She miscarried once more. This time, it was much earlier along. She never spoke of it; upon a later revelation, she would just say it wasn't meant to be. It hurt to realise that we would never be parents. When I use parents in this context, I am referring to blood. I eventually accepted it.

For the next decade and some, we continued with our lives. Maybe not to expectations, but to the best of our abilities. Reflecting on that period, I have since realised those events played a significant role in our lives, much more than either of us realised.

I'm quite confident in saying that we all have heard in our lives, the expression 'time heals all wounds'. What is time? Isn't time merely a concept created by humanity for our convenience? Time doesn't heal. It makes is possible to bury the pain and for the memories to fade. Nevertheless, nothing is truly forgotten.

Chapter 9

Since the death of our child, the years rolled by. Dee and I were living life, happy and in love. Riveting, I know, that is why I am sparing you the middle years, or maybe I should call them the lost years!

What's important is that even when hardship fell upon us, we didn't give up on each other. Unfortunately, I've seen too many people walk away from a relationship for less, only to return in time, wanting to re-kindle what they had and what they threw away. Love and relationships are work, but the work is worth it!

Anyway, our world would soon be turned upside down once again during the spring of 2014.

I remember the events and the period graphically, as if it happened but a few hours ago. What I am about to share may trigger some. Everyone's entitled to an opinion and their feelings without prejudice. Believe me, there were many opinions circulating at the time.

To begin, my uncle revealed his cancer diagnosis, and ultimately, he was fighting a losing battle. I know it may sound harsh and bleak, but it was the reality he and his family were facing. The specialists involved provided their express views of life expectancy, but does anyone truly know? He had periods of difficulties. He lived and enjoyed each day, something we identify when death impacts us. It is when faced with mortality, do we reflect and begin to live. We're all living on borrowed time; no one knows when that day may arrive. Live life how you want and love passionately with your heart and soul, for shared experiences and memories with someone you love are incomparable.

Anyhow, that wouldn't be the only event of the year.

We would learn of Mum willingly admitting herself to the Emergency Department. To provide some insight, we need to venture back a few years to when Mum experienced lower abdominal discomfort. Dee having a medical background and contacts convinced Mum to see a GP. She suspected that Mum's discomfort could be that of her appendix. Mum would see two GPs and having described the symptoms, the first GP recommended her to consume bananas, believing it to be a specific ailment, which makes no sense according to the symptoms presented. The second GP recommended she take Buscopan, an over-the-counter medication, used to relieve cramping of the stomach, bladder and intestines. Dee was far from impressed with their lack-lustre findings and monitored Mum herself. Mum's symptoms would ease for about a week before escalating one morning. An ambulance was called and after some hands on examinations and the presentation of symptoms, the paramedics believed it was potentially her appendix and recommended a trip to the Emergency Department.

Mum's high tolerance for pain was noted with the paramedics, and yet, not passed along or ignored by the Emergency Department doctors. Skipping ahead after her admittance and first examination, where administered oral painkillers. An Emergency Department doctor returned about an hour after the initial examination to perform a second physical examination, where he pressed along her abdomen and the appendix. Although Mum winced, she didn't make a sound. When asked, she rated the pain on the standardised scale (1–10, 10 being excruciating), a three. Fortunately, I was present for the moment, overhearing the doctor discussing Mum's condition with a few others on duty. Their belief, the appendix wasn't a likely candidate, based on Mum's lack of reaction and that further time was necessary to perform additional tests and scans. For the sake of privacy, I will not mention the rest of the discussion. My dad had been by Mum's side from the beginning and he was becoming frustrated with the lack of urgency shown, and understandably so. He confronted a doctor and asked of the risk involved with a ruptured appendix and of the time before peritonitis becomes a serious issue! Again, the doctor dismissed the idea it was the appendix, and if it wasn't for what I call a stroke of fortune, the situation could have been much different. Fortunately, another experienced doctor overheard the discussion and intervened. He came to overrule the other doctor, ordering that Mum be transferred to the operating theatre immediately.

So, if the appendix was not of concern; why did the intervening doctor determine it to be the appendix?

It was a long and anxious wait for all of us. Any surgery runs the risk of complications and/or worse. How time barely inches in such moments. The specialist/surgeon eventually appeared to discuss Mum's surgery and recovery status. She revealed Mum's appendix had ruptured, leaving quite the mess, which she reassured they had cleaned thoroughly, and the placement of a drain, which would remain in place until the fluids ran clear. In addition, she had been started on a course of antibiotics.

Although the outcome was positive, it still failed to sit well with us. If concerns weren't raised and for the fortunate intervention of another doctor, the day may have ended in tragedy.

Returning to that fateful spring day. Names shall be withheld, events, and conversations will be omitted for a magnitude of reasons. If I could share the details in their entirety, I would not hesitate.

Dee and I remained with Mum and Dad as they awaited the ambulance's arrival. For Mum to ask for an ambulance, she was definitely in pain and concerned. She didn't look well. Never had I seen her in such a state, even the appendicitis. The look in Dee's eyes filled me with concern. With the combination of Dee's eyes and Mum's appearance, a feeling of dread overcame me. The paramedics eventually arrived to perform an in-field examination. They recommended Mum go to the hospital. Mum agreed and Dad joined her in the ambulance. They would make their way to an alternate hospital, having been re-routed due to overcrowding and extended wait times at the primary hospital. I mustn't forget, as the paramedics exited the house, Dee made it known they need to pay close attention to her abdomen. She had a suspicion, or at least, there was a possibility Mum could have a twisted or ruptured bowel. As we watched from the window, the ambulance pull out and away from the kerb and into the desolate street, I turned to look at the kitchen table. Sat on a coaster was Mum's mug of tea with a slice of lemon floating. This was when I realised, Mum wouldn't be coming home. The coldest of chills traversed my body before the numbness settled. Intuition can be a blessing, and it can be a curse.

Dad's first call provided next to no information. Arriving at the alternate hospital's Emergency Department, it was quiet and yet, Mum was made to wait at least thirty-minutes before being admitted. He mentioned calling again once she was seen. This call fired Dee up! I hadn't seen her in this state for many years. She would continue to repeat how emergency medicine is time critical. The faster the patient is seen, the better the chance of a favourable outcome. As she exclaimed, in this very instance, was an example of time wasted. I tried everything I could to calm her, but she was so infuriated.

Dad's next call would come through about an hour after the first. A doctor glanced over Mum's paperwork, asking her to describe her symptoms, one being the difficulty to walk, another, radiating pain down both legs (I have omitted a few critical symptoms intentionally) and requested of Mum, a urine sample, having pointed her in the restroom's direction. Scans recommended and ordered. Dad was advised to take the opportunity to return home if he lived nearby as the scans would likely take a while. Having arrived in the ambulance, he was stranded. I jumped in the car, making the short trip to the hospital, which was a faster trip being a quiet weekend morning.

As I arrived, Dad was outside waiting. Once settled in, he explained in great detail of what unfolded that morning. One particular moment he mentioned; of the doctor's gathering around a desk/station, complaining and laughing of the number of geriatrics seen over the course of the night/morning. Clearly audible to all present in the

Emergency Department. And this is acceptable behaviour? He highlighted how two doctors had been mistaken for patients. None on duty had any form of identification visible. At the time of Mum's admittance, there were two other patients. Dad relayed the concern of Dee pertaining to the abdomen and made sure they were aware of Mum's high tolerance to pain. At the time of her admittance, her pain was a nine. Now, if you remember the ruptured appendix, her rating was well at the other end of the scale. He mentioned what Mum disclosed to the doctor of her symptoms, including her abdominal pain, flanking pain and her difficulty to stand, walk or sit.

Three-quarters of the way home and Dee called. She provided us with a nice surprise! We were to return to the hospital as Mum had been discharged. Dad and I were absolutely confused, as well as Dee! Why the hell would the hospital send him home if they were only to discharge her less than ten minutes later? As well as I knew Dee, her tonality indicated she had now passed the point of furious! I turned the car around and headed back to the hospital.

As we arrived, there was Mum, waiting by the sliding doors of the Emergency Department. Having pulled into a pickup bay, Mum started to walk, but stopped, before leaning against the short wall. Dad jumped out to escort and settle her. Mum was strong, proud, and an independent woman. To see her in this condition, appearing weak and dishevelled was gut-wrenching. That sight, the determining factor…I wasn't taking her home; I was taking her to the other hospital, where she should have gone to begin. Mum made her way into the left rear passenger seat with Dad's guidance. Dad would make his way into the front seat. As he was making his way, I looked over my shoulder and asked Mum, what happened? The following are her exact words, which revealed the level of pain she was enduring. "See GP...have MRI." That definitely wasn't Mum. She was an eloquent orator, she could use some choice language at times, but we all do. I asked her for the discharge papers and she uttered, "None," only to hand over a referral for an MRI and a prescription. I was livid over the treatment she received, absolutely disgusted. Once Dad had his seatbelt on, I made sure to slowly depart, making good use of the rear-view mirror to monitor Mum.

Exiting the car park, there was a substantial dip between the drive and the road that shook Mum, provoking a moan from her. Continuing further down the road, entering a roundabout, I noticed Mum had since slumped over her seatbelt. With the car mid-roundabout, I stopped to get out and check on her. Jerking the door open, I checked her pulse, which was weak and thready and sent alarm bells off in my head. In that fraction of a moment, I had to decide whether to call for an ambulance or take Mum back to the hospital. Ultimately, I would floor it back to the hospital. In that time, being less than two minutes, I reached behind and started shaking and slapping her leg hard; yelling for her to focus on my voice and to keep her eyes open. As an added worry, I had Dad. I didn't need two patients on my hands. When I took my first-aid course, I knew I would use the knowledge, but hoped it was for minor injuries. It was imperative to have Mum remain conscious, otherwise the situation would escalate rapidly.

I'm thankful for the quiet weekend roads. The lack of traffic made the run through red lights easier, though still dodgy.

Only a few hundred metres from the hospital; Mum lost consciousness, and I knew I couldn't have Dad become aware, so I continued in the manner I was.

Having pulled into the hospital once again and spotting an ambulance preparing to leave, I instructed Dad to grab a paramedic. I attended to Mum. Opening her door, I leaned in, reaching across her to unbuckle the seatbelt. She had slumped over on the latch; leaving me to forcefully pull her into an upright position and off the buckle/latch. As I re-positioned myself to gain the leverage I would need to drag her out, my ear positioned near her mouth. It was this moment, not only did I hear Mum's final breath; I felt it against my face. For those who may not know, the last breath has a distinct rattle. I released my grip and checked her pulse…nothing. It was then a paramedic entered through the opposite door, checking Mum's pulse and immediately yelling "Code 2!" It was within a few seconds, the other paramedic, along with doctors and nurses, arrived on scene.

Stepping back to clear myself from the area, they dragged Mum's lifeless body from the car and into the kerb. As Mum lay there, I could see her abdomen enlarged. They performed compressions while awaiting the stretcher. They lifted her onto the stretcher and rushed into Resus. As they were rushing her inside, I looked behind to see Dad, standing there…a shadow of the man I knew…shattered.

Dad would follow them in and I would remain to gather Mum's clothing and glasses from the kerb before joining Dad. Gathering Mum's items, it hit me…she was gone.

As I write this in reflection, I'm amazed how composed I remained. It was back in my senior year of high school I undertook my first-aid certification (refresher courses since) and I remember my instructor mentioning, "You may have the knowledge, but until you are in a situation, you will never know if you'll be able to act." I had doubts; I wondered if I would retain the copious knowledge handed down. All that knowledge seemingly flooded my memory, as if stored in a reserve part of my mind. Once that knowledge kicked in, Mum was no longer Mum; she was now someone in need of help. People who've asked me about the events find it difficult to conceive. Maybe it has something to do with my introverted nature or the manner in which I think, *I don't know.* I know I could separate my relationship and emotions from the situation. All I will say is, unless you're thrown into such a situation, it is difficult to leave comment.

Entering Emergency and as I headed towards Resus, I was abruptly stopped and pulled to the side by the Triage nurse and informed bluntly, I was required to divulge the accounts of what unfolded from the time Mum left the hospital to the moment returning in seek of help. She asked a series of questions, only to cut me off each time mid-sentence. All I will say; she ignored valuable information. Having been pardoned, I mean excused; I joined Dad. I mentioned of my experience with the Triage nurse and he went on to describe of his rude encounter with her earlier in the morning when they first arrived.

I know I cannot declare a death, but I knew Mum was gone. The sound of her final breath is a sound I'll always remember and, tragically, I would hear it in the future. Also, at the time of her last breath, I no longer felt her presence. It's hard to explain, but when you are around someone, especially someone you love and/or have known for a long time, you can feel their presence, or maybe energy is a better choice of word. What I felt was a void.

I struggled, whether to say anything to Dad. Ultimately, I kept what I knew to myself. Seriously, how the hell could I tell him that the love of his life was dead? With my emotions high and absorbing his emotions, I couldn't be around him for my sake. I wandered the corridors outside the waiting room, before calling Dee. She knew before I even said a word. Her words, "Mum's gone." It broke my heart to hear her say that. I wanted…I needed Dee more than ever. I still needed to make a few other calls. Never did I conceive I would be in this position. How do you break the bad news? School doesn't teach you and life doesn't teach until it throws you into that very position. The first call to my aunt. I didn't beat around the bush. I simply told her that Mum had likely gone into cardiac arrest and was at the hospital and it didn't look good. She didn't believe me. She thought I was joking. Having taken a moment and hearing the shakiness in my voice as I explained the events of trying to save Mum, the brutal reality set in.

What horrible timing, as her husband was battling cancer and her sister and emotional support, was now dead, although she wasn't aware. 2014 was definitely turning into a year that we'd rather forget.

The next call, to my lifelong neighbours and an extension of the family, in essence. Dee had filled them in with the earlier events, but when I mentioned that Mum likely entered cardiac arrest, they were in disbelief and left wondering, how did it escalate so quickly? Something many would come to wonder.

Having finished the calls I could muster the composure, I noticed a social worker in the waiting room with Dad. Seeing the social worker confirmed what I already knew. To be blunt, it aggrieved me to see such a sight. It must have been that of divine intervention, for at that moment, a nurse appeared in the corridors to ask if I needed any help or could she organise anything. Although Mum's death wouldn't be declared for at least a further hour; I asked if she could arrange for a priest to deliver Last Rites. She gave me a peculiar look, one that I would describe as being surprised...someone discovering another person knowing a secret they thought only a select few knew. She would see what she could do. At least, ten to fifteen minutes had lapsed before her re-appearance. What's to follow further raises questions. She informed me no priests were available to perform Last Rites. Seriously, not a single priest available; out of the many parishes? Either the nurse failed, or the abysmal run of the church and the plague of scandals continued. Hence, Mum did not receive Last Rites, at least by the church, and that angered me! To this very day, I do not know who should bear the fault, but no matter, if a dying person or family requests Last Rites, then Last Rites should be honoured.

Blankly staring through the dirty glass of the sliding doors, out into the car park, I spotted my sister and Dee making their way towards the hospital and the Emergency Department.

As Dee walked through the doors partitioning Emergency from Resus, we simply held each other. There was no need for words, as tears and the events of the day brought back memories of years past. Being in her arms brought comfort, easing the tensions within. In time, I would explain the events as they had unfolded. Her blood was boiling. At that point, I did not know if I could restrain her if she launched an all-out verbal attack. Then again, would I have stopped her? To calm herself, she sat with Dad. As she sat with him, the doors to Resus opened as a doctor emerged, making their way into the waiting room. Body language never lies, always pay attention, for there are always clues. The clue here...it was that of delivering the news that Mum had passed away.

Life had changed once more. Dee would eventually emerge to let me know what was said and we could see Mum, once the police had finished their enquiries. For us, this was a shock...police involved and a line of enquiries! Apparently, this was normal under the circumstance; a healthy patient being discharged to die soon after leaving the care of the hospital. That maybe protocol, yet it still doesn't diminish the feeling that my father and I were suspects in Mum's death. It would be another thirty to sixty minutes before a constable would give the all clear to the immediate investigation.

A few hours after arriving at the hospital in seek of medical care, Mum would be dead. Therefore, I find it so important to live life how you want to enjoy it and when you love, love with all your essence, for life is fleeting. Anyhow, we made our way into Resus. Mum was on the farther side, a white sheet draped across her, her left hand and head exposed. Let me add, while in the room, the social worker and constable were required to be present as an active investigation was technically in place. The social worker instructed us that no items on the body could be removed and to keep all touches in view. What immediately captured my attention and Dee's was that of the enormous size of Mum's abdomen. Her appearance was that of a morbidly obese person, people you see in documentaries. That wasn't Mum; that was a sign. Dee didn't hold back! The first words to cross her lips were that of 'something had ruptured, anyone can see that!' Mum's entire bodies' blood had drained and pooled within her abdomen. Dee would further add; "I told the paramedics something was wrong with her abdomen. No one f...listens! That is why she is lying on the table!"

Over the next couple of hours, each one of us said our last goodbye under the watchful eye of the social worker and constable.

It was surreal.

Dad required some things from home. My sister and I made the trip. Returning to the house...it was just sombre. Approaching the front door, I felt the numbness, and the silence was deafening. Opening the door, the emotions hit hard, decades of memories returning; knowing that she would never grace this house, her home, again. Her mug, still on the table. I scooped out the lemon before pouring the cold tea down the sink. At that moment, I felt Mum's presence. I knew she was in a good place and that her father would have been waiting to welcome her. I collected what Dad needed and returned to the hospital. On the return journey, I was replaying the events relentlessly, analysing every detail as if I was in the editing room, scrubbing through the footage. At the hospital, having to walk past my car and the very spot where Mum died only fuelled my emotions. The rest of the family had arrived, but I just couldn't be in the same room...the collective emotions were unbearable.

By day's end, Dee and I were holding each other. I had wondered if my reactions were quick enough. Usually, I don't share my thoughts, at least until I'm finished processing. I shared my thoughts with her and she told me to stop thinking about it, for I would only drive myself crazy reliving each moment on replay. She assured me that everything I did, my reactions were quick enough. She mentioned I gave Mum a chance, something that wasn't afforded earlier. "Be proud of what you did because many people would have fallen apart." She mentioned Mum didn't die alone, and that's important. She died with the two men she loved by her side, fighting to save her life, and she would have been proud of my actions.

A beautiful and sweet insight, but the pain wasn't any less bearable.

The months to follow were a living hell, having to learn how to adjust to a life without Mum. Then there was the police/coronial investigation/inquiry, the tactics used by the hospital to prevent staff from providing statements or statements before the deadline. There were further points that I'm not at liberty to discuss.

Just the experience was enough for me to lose faith in an ailing health system and the process of answers and ramifications.

If memory serves me well, I believe my victim impact statement fell on the night before Halloween. I arrived at the police station just before five that afternoon, only to wait a further hour for the constable to appear. The process wouldn't begin until half-past six and I wouldn't leave the police station until one the following morning. Mind you, I had prepared my statement, but for unknown reasons, it wasn't accepted, although the statement I provided featured everything in the statement prepared! Those who provided statements or to later provide statements, spent on average, a couple of hours. I still do not know how I exceeded the average.

Exiting the station was oh so fun! When I arrived, I was lucky to find a parking space. There was no issue now, being the only car on the street. Opposite the station was a reserve, and I parked on that side. There was a streetlight some couple of hundred metres up the road, providing barely any light, just wasting electricity at this point. The night was dark, with little influence of the moon, and eerily quiet. Usually, you hear a car or two off in the distance, an insomniac of a bird and, of course, the odd dog barking. Not on this night! I was not only tired, but agitated, having spent hours sitting in a room providing a duplicate statement! As I crossed the road, I heard a male's voice cry out from the distance. I paid little attention. It wasn't a cry for help, nor was it close. I made it halfway across the road before the yell became aggressive and constant. I glanced up the road, near the only streetlight was a guy flailing his arms and running towards me. Weird shit happens during the wee hours of the morning and I had no plans to be an active participant! Remaining calm, pulling out my keys from my pocket and at the ready, I noticed he was now at a full gait. Well, I had the shorter distance, so I sprinted to the car, unlocked the door and jumped in, locking the doors and starting the car. Immediately, I engaged the high-beam to blind him. With him being illuminated, he looked dishevelled and had a bottle in his grasp. I put the car into gear and took off. As the car was level with him, I turned off the lights so he could not identify the car. Once far enough away, I switched the lights on.

Skipping ahead and not too long before Christmas, the coroner's findings from the investigation/inquiry came to light. Not one of the victim impact statements was reviewed for reasons unknown. The cause of death confirmed and with

Mum merely presenting with four of five key symptoms, it was understandable how those on-call in the Emergency Department that morning may have missed the diagnosis. [On a side note, those four symptoms would later be presented to a GP, a veteran and a physiotherapist, all of whom did not know of the incident and all who recommended urgent medical attention and mentioned the same condition.] Also referenced, based on the hospital records (minus missing discharge papers), even if Mum attended another hospital, it was within reason that she may have had a fifty-fifty chance of survival, but likely, the outcome would have been the same. Interesting, considering they did not afford her a fifty-fifty chance to begin! The hospital could not even provide a scan. From the time she entered that Emergency Department, then having been discharged only a couple of hours later, she was living on borrowed time, more than at any period of her life. They did not afford her the chance of survival.

No person should walk into an Emergency Department and endure what she did! I realise there had been many before her, and I am sure many have followed unfortunately.

Indeed, I haven't disclosed all the information, for reasons stated earlier, and it may also upset people.

With Christmas, a unique atmosphere settled mostly.

Dee conceived a way to pay tribute to Mum. I was unaware of her plan, only realising the significance of the gesture once I saw it. Dad and my niece would eventually realise after seeing it. However, I cannot say the same for the rest in attendance. Mum would always be on her feet, cooking at Christmas. She loved to cook and entertain, but it always took a great deal of effort to convince her to sit down and enjoy the day; allowing someone else to do what was needed.

But, that was Mum, old school. There were some Christmases where we would have a victory, albeit a small one, as she would be back at it five to ten minutes later. Dee had set a place for Mum at the table, leaving it empty. It was not only a sweet and compassionate gesture that was born not only from respect, but from honour and love. I never expected those absorbed in their egos to recognise such a gesture when lacking empathy. The only way you learn how to be empathetic is observing the world that not only in which you live, but exist.

I realise that previous paragraph will create a stir.

On top of all that unfolded, I doubt any of them realised the pain Dad was enduring. In the space of a few weeks, he celebrated his forty-fifth wedding anniversary, his birthday and watched on helplessly, as the love of his life died before his very eyes.

Dee was furious…being Christmas, she bottled up her frustrations while everyone gathered for the first Christmas without Mum. Ah, she let it all out afterwards… hoping… hoping they would at least have a shred of humanity lingering within their souls.

Mum was the pillar of the family. I am sure other families out there have one such person who is their pillar. The one, unremarkably strong, independent, compassionate, empathetic, and loving. The one who brings and unites the family.

Since her death, everything has changed, and yet, everything remains the same!

To add to a tragic year, my uncle would lose his battle to cancer, about a week before Christmas. From all accounts, he seemed to be well. Out of the blue, he took a turn and passed away.

I'm aware some of you may think, here he goes again. That is okay, but I will still mention the importance of life's fragility. If you don't wish to read any further, jump ahead to the next chapter.

Life is short, as it is fragile and unpredictable. In the space of a couple of months, I would not only discover that, but learn via a crash course. Life is of lessons derived from our successes and our failures. I have since decided to no longer concern myself with what others may or may not think of me or want me to do with my life. My life is not about living a life that's dictated by others. It is about living a life I enjoy, with the person I love most, and sharing those moments; creating a lifetime of memories. Life is far too fleeting to leave things unsaid and to live with regret. Speak from the heart, don't be afraid to express your emotions and live.

I'd rather been seen as too nice and repulse people because they don't believe or are sceptical, rather than an arsehole that people swoon over.

Chapter 10

Five years have since passed. Five years...it's been difficult to digest that so much time has passed and yet, it seems as if the events transpired yesterday.

Within the year, Dee and I would celebrate our twentieth wedding anniversary. Twenty years...twenty-two, if you count those years of discovery. It's still difficult to fathom, for I never contemplated marriage. For the majority, we had great times, and we had our tough moments. However, we always knew not to say anything in the heat of the moment, for the words expressed maybe forgiven, but never forgotten. We followed that expression, making sure cooler heads prevailed while communicating and listening; always found a path to resolution. A relationship is of constant work and the reward...it's worth it! Like a flower, a relationship needs to be fed and nurtured; otherwise it will fade and eventually die.

My advice: be open, communicate, appreciate, flirt, adore, support, respect, care, champion and love one another. Also, fight for each other. If you are a lover, then you are a fighter. Times will be tough, there is no disputing that, but it doesn't mean you throw in the towel. If you can easily walk away, then the relationship was built on the foundation of lust. Love is something wonderful between two people and you just don't know if you'll experience it again. So, don't waste the opportunity you have over trivial matters.

Call me what you will, but the power of love is truly amazing. Two people who unconditionally and selflessly love each other, there is little they cannot withstand nor achieve.

Although our twentieth wedding anniversary, it also marked the twentieth anniversary of our child's death.

There'd be further upheaval lurking in the shadows, patiently waiting for an opportunity to arise. Late the previous year, Dee experienced some hip discomfort and some pain in her leg. The pain she would describe as sciatic like. She started with specific exercises designed to ease sciatic pain and not too long after, her pain subsided, eventually fading in a couple of weeks. She continued with the exercises. Her relief, however, would be short-lived, with the pain returning. The difference with the re-occurrence, she was now limited to the distance she could walk before having to physically rest and the sharpness of the pain. That limitation would quickly progress, leading her to rest after prolonged periods of standing. We agreed it was more that sciatica; thus making a trip to the GP. She was checked for signs of a hernia and other potential issues, only to have them ruled out, thus warranting further investigation. An ultrasound, ordered. With a referral in her possession and a stroke of luck; along our way home, literally just a few hundred metres, we passed a newly opened imaging business. While waiting for the traffic lights, Dee noted the number and once home, made the call. She would wait a week for her appointment, that being the earliest of any relatively close.

In that week, her condition deteriorated to a point where she became reliant on a walking stick.

Having arrived for the ultrasound, I was watchful over her, making sure she didn't push herself (as strong willed as she was) and being there to support her in the event her leg should buckle. Some believe my actions were that of smothering; that is your opinion. To me, I was supporting and caring for the woman I loved. The ultrasound was over relatively quick with little strain placed upon her. Usually, once complete, you're notified to expect a call once the results are ready. However, on this day, Dee was asked to wait. The sonographer soon would appear, expressing her concern over the inability to define the targeted area, and insisted she undergo a contrasting CT scan. She wouldn't have to wait long, as the sonographer took it upon herself to contact our GP and requested the immediate facsimile of her referral. As we waited, Dee was required to consume a cup of the ever-so appetising contrasting solution! How in the world can anyone stomach that vile solution is baffling! Just the appearance… and the odour had my stomach churning. I can, with confidence, say that there is no way I could keep it down. Dee beside me was pulling faces with each gulp that she somehow swallowed. She consumed it all and kept it down. For that, I praise her!

Around three-quarters of an hour in, the fax machine sprung to life with her referral. I helped her down the long corridor for her CT. I wasn't able to pass beyond the blue doors and remained behind in the corridor. Being quiet and the acoustics of the room and corridor, I could hear the conversation between the technician and Dee. The topic, her inability to place her leg and hip flat, something the sheer pain prevented her from achieving. She made that quite clear, even suggesting a couple of possibilities. Each time the technician attempted to physically adjust her leg, her agonising screams echoed! And yet, there was nothing I could do, other than pace the corridor. It took a while to grab a clear scan, as her leg begun uncontrollably convulsing, due to the pain.

She walked in under her own power, but needed me as additional support for the journey home.

The call came through notifying Dee her scans were ready. Before I could get a foot out the door, she insisted she was tagging along. Who am I to stop her? I knew Dee too well at this point.

Dee remained in the car, while I ran in to grab the scans. The sonographer handed them over, issuing a directive to immediately attend our GP, as he was expecting Dee's arrival. To hear those words, your mind determines that the urgency expressed equates to a potentially serious issue.

As we waited in the GPs office, her hand in mine, the GP entered, explaining how on her pelvic bone, a lesion detected. The cause and type of lesion was unknown and required further investigation. The GP handed Dee a letter and instructed her that once she left his office; she was to head directly to the Emergency Department and to make sure Triage reviews the letter.

SPOILER ALERT: No script writer could conceive the events that would unfold from this point onwards. I'm borrowing the line above from a person I would meet later who had over a decade of experience dealing with the health system.

Once again, because of legal and privacy reasons, names and places have been withheld, and some events omitted.

We arrived at the Emergency Department early afternoon; it wasn't what I would call busy. About two hours, possibly more, passed before Dee would be seen. With my help, she made her way into the Emergency Department itself. With no bays/beds available, she was required to have her examination undertaken in a paediatric room, where nurses would traverse. She underwent a series of physical examinations and asked a series of general and specific questions before her blood drawn. After the completion of the physical examination, the doctor spoke with her, mentioning what she believed it to be and that the current hospital did not specialise in the treatment of such a condition. (I would find that remark interesting.) The doctor would speak with a colleague at another hospital specialising in such conditions and relevant information, to be included in her discharge papers.

It sounded quite promising.

It was time to rejoin the public, herded back into the waiting area and the waiting game continuing once more. Dee would be called into the office of the Triage nurse, where her blood pressure recorded. Hobbling back and struggling to find a comfortable position, she would come to find a position that didn't cause too much pain and as Murphy would have it, she was called for an x-ray just as she found comfort. Carefully assisting her, we made the long, strenuous and painful walk to the x-ray area. Once complete, they provided her with a wheelchair, and I became the unpaid and uninsured orderly. I was issued strict instructions to follow the coloured lines on the floor, for the lines would guide us to the waiting area. If you are wondering why I was the one pushing her; staff shortages. The lines had faded in areas, making following a specific colour a tad challenging, if it wasn't for common sense and paying attention to the positioning of the lines. Further time passed before she would be at it again, this time a CT. Unlike the x-ray, I would be the one pushing the wheelchair, guided by a nurse out in-front. By the time her scans were complete, we returned to the waiting area and to the amber hue of the setting sun. All the up and down and waiting, becoming agitating for Dee. I approached Triage and asked about the whereabouts of her discharge papers. I was politely informed the doctor would need to see her again. At least, another forty-five minutes before the doctor re-emerged, calling for Dee. This time, she was seen in an Emergency Department bay. It was at this precise moment when Dee was handed over and into the care of another doctor. The new doctor approached, introducing himself by surname only. Dee was subjected to answering the same series of questions asked of her earlier. On this occasion, no physical examination. Intriguing! From the Emergency Department bay, Dee was then transferred to the Short Stay Unit to make room in Emergency.

The waiting game would continue in the Short Stay Unit. As the name applies, you feel there would be more focus on reducing waiting times. Dee's new doctor would re-appear to inform her of the lesion present on her pelvic bone, could be of an infection or cancer. He handed her a pamphlet to browse, while informing her she would require a bone density scan and an MRI, both of which the hospital did not service. With her physical limitations, he recommended she find an imaging place that provided both services to reduce stress. Finally, he clarified she needed to set up an appointment with the head of orthopaedics at their private office as soon as she secured a date for her scans.

Not what anyone wants to hear the word cancer and that the hospital, a large hospital, cannot perform a bone scan or

MRI. I would query Dee regarding the first doctor, the referral, the discharge and that this hospital could not treat such a condition and yet, here she remained. Then adding the second doctor's contradiction; referring her to the head of orthopaedics. We had concerns, and I tried to locate the elusive doctor to express our concerns; not even the nurse's station could pin him down.

The day morphed into night and becoming long in the tooth. It seemed as Dee had become forgotten, left to deal with the pain and discomfort whilst eaten by the many mosquitoes calling the Short Stay Unit home. This now past the ridiculous and entered the sublime territory. Dee arrived just after two in the afternoon and it was now past nine in the evening. Having approached the nurse once more, and as I arrived; she informed me Dee's discharge papers were currently in the print queue. After an additional five to ten minutes, I was handed two envelopes containing Dee's discharge papers. With a very early GP appointment, she could finally go home and try to get some rest and ease her pain.

As I expected, she had a restless night.

The following morning, we received some shocking news. Having examined both envelopes, our GP shared the colossal error made by the hospital. The papers in both envelopes were not of her discharge, but the discharge of an elderly male of different ethnicity presenting with significantly different symptoms. How does a hospital screw up a patient's discharge? He instructed us to contact the hospital immediately to rectify the mess. In the meantime, Dee shared the information provided the night before, leaving the GP baffled why the hospital could not perform at least the MRI, considering there's an MRI at the hospital.

Once home, I helped to settle Dee in and made sure she was comfortable. I called the hospital to speak with the liaison office; explaining the situation. According to the system, the discharge was incorrect. She should not have been discharged, as she had an outstanding blood work order. After some further investigation, a rush issued, with the head of the department duly notified. Once the blood work was complete, her discharge would be signed and posted.

The entire process took a staggering thirty-one days! Yes, you read that number correctly, thirty-one days! A month after admittance to the Emergency Department, did she receive the correct discharge papers. This is not an exaggeration and I will repeat the sentiment of Dee. Emergency medicine is time critical!

While on the phone with the hospital, Dee secured her appointment for her scans and with the head of orthopaedics.

Her condition continued to worsen each day. I put forward our concerns to our GP and his inability to act as the system had his hands bound. Dee's primary carer was the head of orthopaedics, the specialist she had yet to meet. The walking stick, no longer beneficial; Dee reliant on crutches. Her range decreased considerably, being forced to rest after five to ten metres of walking. I fought hard to keep my emotions in check. To see her, a once active woman now but a shell of herself, only able to hobble but a few metres. I couldn't imagine the pain she was enduring and there she was, continuing to fight.

The day of her scans, it was a nightmare. The imaging business, like most, provided no parking and the surrounding streets full, with the only spot involving a lengthy walk for her. The only positive was that of a small brick wall that ran most of the length. She would be able to stop and rest along the way. The walk involved would take an average able person between three to five minutes, but Dee, it took over twenty-five minutes, not including the rests. She pushed herself at points, not wanting to be late and miss her appointment. Rounding the corner and approaching the entrance, it presented her with another challenge. She would need to overcome four steep steps and a small ascent to the landing. I offered to carry her, but she wouldn't entertain the thought, refusing to concede her independence sooner than she may have to. She was a strong and independent woman, only a couple of the many things I loved about her, and I wasn't about to deny her. Instead, I positioned myself closely behind, observing her every movement and ready to jump in and assist if the moment arrived. She climbed those stairs with fierce determination and without hesitation. I was proud of her!

What was now becoming second-nature, once inside the office, I settled her before approaching reception. Without revealing details, there was a lengthy holdup when the referring specialist could not be found in the system, or didn't have privileges at the nominated hospital. Quite interesting when the specialist was the head of orthopaedics! The staff found a creative work-around to the problem; otherwise, Dee's scans would have been in limbo until the situation rectified. With what had already happened, who knows the time it would have taken? And when I say rectified, I mean myself or Dee chasing the issue.

As we quickly discovered through this ordeal, the onus is solely on the patient's shoulders.

By the way, how uncomfortable are the seats in the waiting rooms?

As we waited, which was becoming quite common, and probably an activity I could list as a pastime. I couldn't help to but notice the posters plastered on the walls. Every second one was a public notice to switch off mobile phones. The posters weren't hard to miss, but when you're not observant, even the obvious remains unseen. So, it was quite amusing and concerning to see the few other people waiting with their faces planted in their phones, occasionally diverting their eyes, but not so sure of their attention. There was one man in particular, so focused on his phone; oblivious to his name called some four times. It was on the fifth occasion where a staff member physically approached him to grab his attention, and then, he didn't offer an apology for his actions.

Dee's MRI; anticipated to take an hour at most, would exceed the hour, stretching for a further thirty minutes. It isn't difficult to conclude why. The technician invited me in towards the final five minutes, primarily to assist Dee. Next, the bone density scan, and from our understanding, there would be a two stage process involved. The receptionist was kind to let us know Dee had a little over an hour before her scan and suggested taking the time to grab a bite of lunch if we desired. Dee might be hungry, but I wasn't, so I asked her. I would at least grab a bottle of water or two. She wasn't hungry, but wanted to get out of the building. Helping her to her feet, handing her the crutches, the receptionist asked us to follow her. So, we followed her down the corridor and to the rear of the building, where she opened a large rolling door. This would help us; Dee not having to navigate stairs. The receptionist told us to press the doorbell when we returned, and someone would open the door. I wish they made this known prior to our arrival, but a compassionate gesture none the less and one appreciated.

We made the slow journey around and to the various mixed businesses. I bought Dee a juice and a water to keep her hydrated. As usual, she noticed I bought nothing for myself and she gave me her infamous look of dissatisfaction. I wasn't important; I know my limits and how far I can push those limits. My priority was her and only her. She stood for a bit, eventually needing to take a seat. I stood as I usually do. I'm not one for sitting, preferring to stand, and that can unsettle some. We chatted for a while, sharing in some memorable moments that not only brought smiles to our faces, but the long absent sound of laughter. I couldn't remember the last time I saw her smile or laugh. The chatter soon moved to the serious, acknowledging the possibility of her and our end may very well be nearer than we realise. It's not a topic anyone wants to discuss, but you cannot continue to bury your head in the sand either. Our time is fleeting; our expiration begun the moment we were conceived. Unfortunately, the majority know not of their end. I know it sounds quite grim, but with the mishaps and errors stemming from the hospital and her continuing deterioration, we both knew the end was closer to any other time prior. We had to acknowledge that probability. Although we acknowledged it, it didn't imply that either of us had conceded the fight. We still had hope, and we still had plenty of fight. You just need to be prepared, and with Dee's background and resources, she was well aware of the gravity of the situation at hand. She may have tried to hide it, but when you truly know someone, you develop additional senses in relation to them. You cannot simply hide yourself away, no matter how you may try.

We returned, making sure we dedicated ample time for the arduous walk, returning as we left, via the 'secret' entrance.

Knowing her bone scan was on the second level, we noticed the lack of an elevator. This could become quite interesting! Fortunately, no climbing or carrying was required. One of the receptionist staff climbed the dimly lit stairs before sending down a mobility chair. Dee was helped into the chair and strapped in. I was handed her crutches, and the receptionist sent the chair up and onwards before scurrying past Dee to await her arrival. I would follow soon after with crutches in hand, passing her around the halfway point and having a chuckle with her as I passed her with little effort.

Her scans took in-excess of two hours to complete. The initial scan that was referred to as the referencing scan was quick. The second was that of the detailed scan. While she underwent the scan, I waited in the cold and dimly lit corridor. I would have at least paced the length of that corridor a couple of hundred times. As I paced, I could only think of the battle ahead for her and was optimistic she would stamp her authority to fend off and defeat the challenge issued by the cancer. Yes, we believed with her rapid deterioration, the visual signs and other factors, it was cancer. I thought of the discharge papers (still a couple of weeks from arriving) and what was contained in those papers, particularly the first doctor's remarks. However, without the papers, we were flying blind.

And yes, we had spoken of the notion of another hospital. We'd be required to go through the process again. The referral would be quick from our GP, the new scans might be faster, but might take a month or longer and then returning to the GP to be referred to the hospital, this time, a different hospital and maybe the process is smoother, then again, maybe it's the same. Time is critical and with too many unknown factors, Dee decided she couldn't afford to take the chance of losing further time. I agreed with her and supported her.

I would learn the tortures of waiting during this experience, not knowing of the happenings during the scans. That time waiting allowed my mind to explore all the possibilities, variables and various scenarios; hoping to find a probable or potential solution or to prepare myself. The mind of an over thinking introvert.

With her scans finally complete and her body battered, having gone through hell, it was time to return home and hopefully rest and enjoy the weekend. On our way out, the receptionist made it be known, her results would be available Monday afternoon, not all that long to wait. There's that word I have come to despise…wait!

Dee found little comfort over the weekend. The frequency between her bouts of severe pain was shortening, and the duration increasing. And yet, our GP could only do so much, and the specialist wasn't in the picture. This is the flailing system we and many others contend with.

Moving ahead in the timeline and to the afternoon of Dee's specialist appointment.

Although she had an appointment, she didn't have an appointment. He or maybe I should say, his staff would squeeze her in amongst the many other appointments of the afternoon. The waiting room, jammed packed; Dee was lucky to find a seat. I would make ourselves known to the receptionist, where informed her appointment was not set, but they would squeeze her into the doctor's already busy schedule when workable. Interesting! When is an appointment an appointment? And the use of the word 'workable'! My intuition in that moment…it wasn't positive. Returning, Dee was enjoying a conversation with an older lady. What she would uncover from that conversation was of the specialist's reliable nature of running late and to expect lengthy waits. Life for us had become that of waiting. I wonder if I should add that to my C.V.! We had no reason not to show some faith in what the lady had said, especially seated in the waiting room and seeing it first-hand. Plus, with all that had unfolded so far, it would fit perfectly with the narrative of the story.

Dee would be 'squeezed' in some thirty to forty minutes after her scheduled appointment. However, we must take into consideration the specialist was doing her a favour by squeezing her into his already busy schedule. I handed over Dee's scans to the specialist. After sipping on his coffee and reviewing what I believe to be his notes, he placed the scans on the light box; quickly glancing over them before reviewing the included report. The images were deemed to be lacking of the definitive, and she would require an urgent biopsy. It would be undertaken at the hospital where it all began. All she need do, contact the specialty department and arrange an appointment. To hear the word urgent not only raises eyebrows, it starts the mind thinking. The scans weren't definitive to begin, a second series of scans also returned as not definitive, and yet no sense of urgency. My question, what wasn't being said?

The specialist glanced at the time, to then explain the urgency of the biopsy, mentioning the department would close in a couple of days for the Christmas and New Year's period. It was imperative she call tomorrow morning, as the department was now closed and when securing her appointment, reference the word 'urgent'. In the event she experienced any issues, she was to call his office. Having handed Dee a handwritten referral, he sent on her way.

I must be from an alternative universe. If there is a sense of urgency and being the head of orthopaedics, why is the arrangement of a critical appointment in the hands of the patient, considering the department shuts down for a few weeks? Wouldn't a department head be more likely to organise and secure an appointment, absent of difficulties?

Let's continue this train moving forward and onto the next day. Once that clock displayed 09:00, we were on the phones. As two heads are better than one, so are two phones. You would think to organise an urgent procedure as a biopsy would involve little to no hassle! If you thought along those lines, you are sadly mistaken! The many attempts to only be told the department was closed for Christmas and no appointments available until the New Year and advised to call in the New Year. Okay…within reason of sanity, why wouldn't a person be able to organise an appointment that day for the following year? The department wasn't closed at this point, so I don't understand how an appointment couldn't be made for the following year!

Apparently, the definition of urgent that Dee and I share and likely other people, differs from the definition of the health system. In my disbelief and frustration, I pulled out three different dictionaries and utilised the definition made available online. Apart from the structuring, the definitions were the same. The same definition Dee and I knew and acknowledged. Dee called the specialist's office, explaining the situation. It was now in the hands of the specialist...the head of orthopaedics to come through! *I didn't hold much hope and the more, I thought, I came to realise the lack of clout he had.*

Friday would enter, and the day would end with no appointment! Three days! Three days and nothing! This was the straw that broke the camel's back, with the decision to escalate the issue with the hospital directly. Being that of the weekend, the liaison office was closed. A message left and promptly returned the upcoming Monday. They assured us to expect a call from the department that afternoon. I think you can guess what happened. That's right; the phone didn't ring nor vibrate. Another message left with the liaison office and another call returned the following day and once more, reassured we would receive a call. This time, Dee received her call to confirm her appointment for early January.

She would endure a further three weeks of discomfort, pain, deterioration and stress as the cancer continued to grow. That's right, the 'urgent' biopsy required to identify her condition was still weeks away!

Here we have a patient in severe discomfort and significant pain. Then, the word cancer is dropped, only to add to the patient's stress and concerns. On top of all this, the onus of an urgent procedure is that of the patient's responsibility, not the primary care specialist. Where does any of this make sense?

Today, some years later, I'm still perplexed; how a critical department within a major hospital simply closes for the Festive Season! Can and will anyone shed some fucking light on this? It's the equivalent of a major city Fire Department or Police Force shutting down. Could you imagine the ensuing chaos and outcry if such a move were to happen? But for a hospital, it is acceptable?

The errors continued and now were snowballing out of control! Adding to the situation was the lack of avenues available...there was nowhere she could turn. As I mentioned earlier, it would be a gamble back then to start the process over and even a greater gamble to do so now. She was at the mercy of the system, a broken system, one being held together with band-aids and butterfly clips.

With Christmas rapidly approaching, Dee's most favourite times of the year, I couldn't allow the actions of the system to deny her further. I erected a small tree, pinned a garland and sporadically added some decorations, as well as setting up a projector outside. I wasn't in the mood to celebrate, but I knew she loved it and this moment was not about me. Her condition further deteriorated, and her dependence on me grew evermore. She must have thought she was a burden, but that wasn't true. I loved her and I was in love with her and when you love someone, you'll do anything for that person, no matter the times.

I remember the smile that decorated her face, as the sun set and having positioned the projector to shine through the window and onto the ceiling. The display danced for her to enjoy from the chair that she was now confined. It might not sound like much, but it was a priceless moment. We were unsure if this would be our last Christmas, and yet deep down, we both knew it was.

We remained strong and united, never giving up hope or on each other, for in the absence of hope, there is only despair.

The year without a Christmas…

A Festive Season it may have been, but not for us. We grabbed the opportunity to spend as much time together, unearthing some old objects as we reminisced about the moments associated. Dee became so excited when I found one of her earlier mobile phones that she absolutely adored! That excitement only escalated when the phone powered on! It had been years. The battery was in good physical condition and contained enough of a charge to bring it back to life. I would also unearth a camcorder cassette that featured our time State side. Fortunately, I still had similar tapes, so I wasn't without a VHS-C to VHS converter cassette. After giving it a dust off, I connected a relic VCR player to the television and loaded the cassette. Ah! The sound of the cassette loading, the scan lines on the TV, and the bouncing image before auto-tracking worked its magic. As the tape played, the memories returned. It was as if it was only yesterday we had been driving past the mill pond, along the country roads, past the corn crops and historical tobacco sheds, all the while enjoying ourselves, without a care for tomorrow. How I would have loved to have been able to flick a switch and return to a much more blissful time, never having to leave that moment, never losing a child, never growing old. But life doesn't work in that manner.

With the New Year, the unbelievable events of the past year, hopefully that, past events! The lesion that started out as a relatively small area on the scans had since grown to become a significant mass, clearly visible to the naked eye and yet, with no avenues available, Dee would continue to suffer unnecessarily.

Aware of Dee's growing struggles, unable to walk, unable to bear weight, pain and fatigue to mention but a few, we arrived at the hospital early for her appointment; we weren't about to take any chances. She was determined to complete the walk without my help. A good sign, for it showed me she hadn't conceded and her fierce fighting attitude was still burning! Although slow, she made it! Part of me was concerned about the after-effects of such a gruelling walk and the other part of me was so proud of what she had just accomplished. I would help her into the unusually low seats of the waiting area before venturing over to reception. I waited ten minutes with no signs of life. Immediately, my thoughts conceiving where this was about to go; proceeding to the other department's receptionists to explain the lack of reception and the need to confirm Dee's appointment. They were quite accommodating, acknowledging the situation, and provided interesting information to why the lack of reception staff. Given an opportunity, people are willingly to divulge information.

Seriously, no script writer could produce such a storyline!

I wasn't about to withhold the news from Dee; as we waited, I filled her in. Without going into detail, both reception staff quit before the Festive Season break, some three weeks earlier. Not only this was concerning, it was another error to add to the growing list. What hopes of a fresh beginning for a New Year had just faded! In that case, who registered Dee's appointment?

I was pissed! My stress levels, likely through the roof. Dee was my focus and what I was experiencing was merely a speck compared to all that she was enduring. I was doing everything I could for her and was losing and ultimately failing her. Losing is one thing and I detest losing, but to fail the person you love, the person who trusts you with their heart and soul, is unbearable as it is inconceivable.

We continued to wait, watching the hands of the clock round the face, until the hands passed her scheduled appointment time. Now, only six people waiting in the area, including Dee. So, I wouldn't say it was busy. Twice, the receptionist informed us, nurses were locating her paperwork. Locating her paperwork...are you fucking kidding me? [I apologise for the obscenities. Usually I refrain from using such words, but when I become passionate, they fly.] How? How have they lost her paperwork, paperwork for an urgent biopsy that should have been done the year prior? If blood could boil within these veins of mine, steam would be visible. My frustration continued. From the back rooms, a nurse appeared, striking up a conversation with the reception staff. Little did she realise, with such an empty and quiet room, the echo and acoustics were superb! I was far from impressed with the remarks made. I am not one to confront, but when pushed, or the situation dictates, I will. Dee had only ever witnessed me reach that point once and on this occasion, she calmed me and convinced me, I would only waste my words.

Two to three hours had passed since her scheduled time. Who was counting? Eventually, a nurse appeared asking Dee to follow her through to an examination room, where a doctor was waiting. The doctor would explain of their inability to locate her paperwork, proceeding to question Dee as if she hadn't an appointment. Now, that was a monumental error made by the doctor! Dee didn't hold back, tearing into him, the department, the specialist, the hospital and the system. She emphasised each error and delay, including today, and emphasised how her biopsy was urgent and should've happened last year. By the end, both the doctor and nurse were apologising and clearly embarrassed. Dee handed over the referral, where it was scanned and a file generated based on a series of questions asked. The doctor would explain the likelihood of the biopsy happening today was highly unrealistic as there were a few patients ahead of her and the Emergency Department patients took preference. Dee was offered Friday of that week or a choice of days the following week. She opted for the Friday, to only be denied, for Friday; designated for full anaesthetic procedures and hers would require but a local. Why offer a day that was unavailable? Her second 'urgent' biopsy was now scheduled a week later. We were far from impressed. Before leaving, Dee made sure the doctor noted that with bouts of pain, not only her heart rate increased, but her blood pressure too.

Leaving, it was obvious the amount of pain she was enduring, and there was nothing I could do to ease it. To feel helpless is horrible, but to know she was feeling helpless just magnified the emotion and sensation.

We couldn't put the hospital behind us; it was impossible. It had become entrenched in our life! We discussed at great length the series of errors and the lack of accountability. Dee was living a horror story! Each turn, her path hindered with errors. The avenues of action were futile or non-existent. She was now deteriorating at her fastest rate. The tumour and not lesion was growing at an astonishing rate. The unrelenting pain, the inability to perform menial tasks we take for granted, feeling helpless and as a burden and, of course, the stress. She didn't need the added stress. Her body was already enduring enough. But error after error, it continued to surmount! I still cannot fathom how she managed! That is why I will always refer to her fight as one of the bravest fights I'd seen. I didn't come out unscathed.

The Friday before her second attempt, I mean appointment; I phoned the hospital to organise the use of a wheelchair. They informed me that only when arriving and only on arrival at the hospital could I organise a wheelchair by approaching the Information Desk.

Time to put the advice and claims into action. Arriving at the hospital an hour early, Dee took a seat opposite the Information Desk as I waited patiently for a few minutes for the two staffers to finish their intense conversation of their weekend frolics. I requested the use of a wheelchair for her, only to be informed it would take at least thirty minutes or more to organise one, but not guaranteed. Well, there was no way we were about to jeopardise her appointment waiting on a wing and a pray. Dee hobbled in agony once more to her appointment. Most people wouldn't realise that with intense pain comes elevated heart rates and blood pressure, but…you would think medical professionals would!

The journey this time was taking a toll, having her stop more frequently. In the space of a week, the walk added an extra fifteen minutes.

Being the second time around, the 'urgent' biopsy looked much more promising. However, I'm not sure if I should use the word urgent considering the time that since lapsed. Dee passed her pre-requisite health check and shown to a waiting room; unbeknown if they would undertake her biopsy for Emergency Department patients took priority. I was instructed to go home and to expect a call where I would receive the details regarding patient pickup procedures. I made it close to halfway home when I received a call from Dee, who just happened to be occupying a bed in the Emergency Department. The doctor in charge of the biopsy requested another round of tests and found her blood pressure and heart rate of concern. Having explained the situation the week prior in relation to the spikes caused through pain and seemingly omitted from her file, she explained the situation furthermore. I had been documenting this cycle for some time. The doctors attempted to control her pressure with the use of a medicated patch or something similar. What was concerning was that of the lack of acknowledgement or addressing from the specialist and the doctors regarding her pain and pain control. Dee would remain in Emergency until later that afternoon, when discharged and instructed to seek the advice and care of her GP to manage her condition.

I can understand the decision not to proceed with the biopsy. Safety is a priority. However, she should not have arrived at this point if her pain had been managed.

With each day, she was deteriorating before my eyes. The cancer (though unconfirmed until a biopsy could take place) was growing, and every error combined with each day of inaction was denying her a chance at survival.

A new day and another unnecessary trip. The GP along with us, frustrated with the situation and the system. The GP placed Dee on a small dosage of blood pressure medication and left to us to monitor and record the results over the course of a week. She would need to return to see if she fell within the parameters set by the hospital.

Her return the following week proved successful. Given the green light, the GP assisted in scheduling her third attempt! She would wait a further week and a couple of days.

Two months had passed since Dee walked into the Emergency Department. Just over a month and a half since she saw the specialist, and informed of the possibility of cancer and the urgency of the biopsy. I will leave it to you; all within a reasonable time frame?

Third time lucky, as they say. The biopsy was a success and while in recovery, the doctor who performed the procedure informed her of the expected soreness over the next couple of days and to avoid unnecessary movement (that wouldn't be an issue). Her results should be ready in two weeks and to make an appointment with her specialist immediately if the specialist hadn't already made an appointment and to check-in with the specialist from the second week onwards to verify her results were in. Of course, she made the appointment and not the other way around. The receptionist informed her that only if the doctor was concerned about the findings would he bring her appointment forward. Now, that piece of information will become relevant soon.

I found it difficult then as I do today. So often you read or hear of the importance of identifying and treating cancer, for the earlier the diagnosis and treatment, the better the odds. That applies to most illness and disease. Of course, there are exceptions to the rule as with anything in this life. During those first two weeks of waiting, reality settled with Dee and it hit me hard. You do everything within your control to remain optimistic, positive and hopeful, but common sense lingers. Dee had me empty our wardrobe, bringing each item to her so she could determine which to keep, to hand down, to donate and which she wanted me to keep. I was fighting to hold back the tears, refusing to cry in-front of her, not for shame or embarrassment; I was her pillar of strength. It was about her fight...her survival! I was there to love and support her. She picked out a few summer items to keep, which was a positive in my eyes. Considering we were heading into winter, her actions spoke loudly. She hadn't given up!

Next on the so-called agenda, me. Dee knew me better than I knew myself. Strange, but true. She spoke of what I needed to do in the event of a poor outcome. I had to promise her that in time, I wouldn't hide myself away and I would open my heart to love again. Do you realise how crushing those words were to hear? I envisioned us growing old together, not either of us needing to say goodbye to the other so early and attempting to piece what shattered life remained back together. No one wants to think, let alone hear, of death and its impact. We also discussed whether a palliative care facility would be an option. We agreed, if that time should arise, then she would spend her remaining time at home. In addition, we discussed who amongst the family would be privy to the results, once known. Dee decided, of course, her employer needed to know and who I must acknowledge. What the company did for her was unbelievable! They truly went above and beyond!

Having now entered the third week, post biopsy, we rotated calls into the office of the specialist. Most days, a call in the morning and again in the afternoon. It wasn't until the end of the third week when the receptionist informed Dee her biopsy results were in. Dee questioned if the specialist had reviewed the results and of the need to bring her appointment forward. She was assured she need not worry about moving her appointment. We were relieved! Not having to move her appointment suggested there wasn't anything of elevated concern. Still, she wasn't out of the proverbial woods, especially if any surgery was required. Nevertheless, our minds found some comfort.

One month to the day of the biopsy (or for those keeping track, around the three-month mark). Dee found a seat in the over-crowded waiting room of the specialist. She was struggling more than ever to walk and to bear weight. As we waited, I received a call that diverted to voicemail due to the loudness of the room. I popped outside quickly to retrieve the message which was from the office of the specialist. It surprised me to have received a call. The message was advising Dee to immediately attend the doctor's office! My first concern; being that of the sudden urgency. My second issue being that of today. Today was her scheduled appointment, a detail they should have been aware! If I could reveal all the details, many would be in disbelief. Sadly, I wish I was embellishing. I'm not. I returned inside and filled Dee in. If looks could kill, then God help anyone she focused her attention on! It wouldn't be long before she would be called. The specialist informed her that only yesterday did he return from holiday and it was not until late afternoon that he had the opportunity to review her results. Upon review, the decision made; to have her brought in immediately. For those paying attention, you should be able to spot the discrepancy or should I say discrepancies! Dee was still as sharp as ever, asking some revealing questions of him. Again, I cannot go into detail.

He revealed the diagnosis of cancer. Something we had concluded some time ago. The official diagnosis was that of Chondrosarcoma. It is not as common as other cancers. He would briefly touch on the basics. One point of great concern was the specialist's inability to treat the condition, thus referring Dee to a colleague working out of another hospital. Coincidently, the hospital she was referred (verbally and later referenced in the discharge) the previous year by the first doctor she interacted in the Emergency Department. The specialist handed her another handwritten referral, instructing her to the receptionist for further information. The interaction provided little information, only to generate another series of delays and errors.

If you've been following along, I think you might conclude what happens next.

The ride home was devastating. There is no other way to describe it. Deep within, we knew the outcome wasn't to favour her. The insurmountable errors and delays…and the odds stacked against her.

Once home, without a moment of hesitation, I began compiling research on this cancer. Chondrosarcoma, not a name easily forgotten. Dee touched base with a couple of friends still in medicine, which was beneficial. Each of her contacts emphasised the imperativeness of treating this cancer quickly, as it wasn't like others. Chondrosarcoma is a slow growing cancer. Now, that doesn't seem all too concerning. The information I uncovered was hopeful, but there was a dark caveat to be confirmed by her contacts. The cancer can become de-differentiated and if it does, life expectancy is poor! In addition, the cancer does not respond to radiotherapy or chemotherapy. The only way to deal with such a beast is to remove the cancer with healthy margins. When Dee mentioned to them how long the entire process to this very point had taken, not only were they concerned, it mortified them.

All we could do was hope it wasn't de-differentiated, but my intuition was telling me to prepare for the worst. Our gut feeling (intuition) is our most primitive instinct and, more often than not, our gut is spot on. Dee would need one hell of a miracle to beat this! The number of errors continued to run through my mind, also the lack of empathy and support. The head of orthopaedics saw her but twice, to organise two referrals and to deliver the results. This specialist was her primary health carer. Our GP experienced difficulties contacting him, just as we had. The observations and records documented by myself and Dee's own accounts, not once considered. She never received a copy of her biopsy results nor our GP, though requests made.

With a week having passed, and yet to receive a call, Dee called her specialist. Her call, placed on hold before receiving the information required. Her referred appointment was set for mid-morning tomorrow, and she was required to confirm with the specialist before her appointment date. Dee's tone said enough! When she asked of the address and contact details, her call, placed on hold, before being terminated. It was now in our hands to track down the contact details of the referred specialist. After some searching, we had the details and Dee called to make the arrangements. The receptionist was pleasant, guiding her through the requirements of her appointment. One being the biopsy results, and Dee explained that could be a challenge. After ending the call, Dee would call her former specialist and request her biopsy results faxed across to the referred specialist, providing the number. She couldn't help but to speak of the contrast between the two offices.

The new specialist, whom from this point onwards shall be known as Dr P.

A few days earlier, an old family friend saved the day, loaning us his wheelchair. This was about to make appointment life much easier for her. The glaring issue at hand was that of the biopsy results. As I previously mentioned, we didn't have a copy, or our GP. The likelihood of Dr P's office receiving a copy…I wasn't confident.

Appointment day…a miserable day, weatherwise. Dee was feeling the best she had in recent memory. The day was overcast, cold, a constant drizzle with the occasional passing shower. The drive was pleasant enough, although a tad long for Dee in her condition, but it was a hopeful opportunity to correct the wrongs of the previous months. Having arrived amid a passing shower, I prepared the wheelchair and, as the shower passed, helped her into the chair. Never would I have imagined what I learnt two decades earlier I would recall and put into practice. Covering her with a blanket and with an umbrella overhead, I pushed her towards the office of Dr P. along the slippery roads and slick footpaths. Upon entering reception, a few details needed my attention. The receptionist pointed us towards the waiting room and once Dee was comfortable; I was to pop back in and fill out the necessities. Apart from Dee and myself, two others were waiting. Quite a stark difference from our previous experience. While at reception I asked if, by any chance, Dee's biopsy results had come through. They checked the pile of faxes and…nothing! They checked their inbox…nothing! Not surprising one iota.

Truly an interesting and different appointment, nothing either of us had experienced prior. Dr P. was quite friendly and warm, introducing himself and establishing a connection and trust. His first question to Dee, "What brought you to me?" Of course, she mentioned the referral. He chuckled to then repeat the question again. This time, she mentioned the cancer along with her pain and limitations. He stopped her there and said, "That's right, pain. Without it, you wouldn't be sitting here in my office." Dr P. asked Dee to hop up on the examination bed; she explained it was impossible. Without missing a beat, he made his way to her in the wheelchair and began his examination. When he needed her to stand, I lifted her and supported her from behind.

Having completed the physical examination, he asked for the biopsy results. We explained the situation, and he wasn't concerned. He picked up the phone, calling the switchboard at his hospital, before connecting with the department at the hospital who performed the biopsy. In less than three minutes, he had the results. That call revealed Dr P's clout and further distinguished the two specialists from one another! He would take the time to explain the reasoning behind the pain as the cancer destroyed her pelvic bone. The scans revealed a significant portion destroyed and without the bone, there was no support and any weight-bearing activities would be near impossible and painful. Dee explained how the situation developed. Dr P. assured her she acted correctly. He explained there was no way for her to know there was anything wrong until she felt that intense pain. Some people are fortunate, as they have scans for unrelated issues that uncover the cancer lurking, usually early. Therefore, considering the results, the scans and her current condition, he made her a priority.

Knowing of her limitations, he would provide a private room at the hospital where all scans would be undertaken, without the need of her travelling, thus reducing further undue stress. The reception team would organise everything. All she needed to do; provide a swab and a blood sample as required by the hospital and to arrive on time.

What a stark difference between the two specialists. I shall leave it at that.

Dee entered the office of Dr P., with the absence of a course of action and left, finally with a plan after months of errors and delays.

Chapter 11

Arriving at the hospital, only to be greeted with a multi-level car park that was far from accessibility friendly was a shock. Albeit, the car park was owned by a private entity. It made for a challenge, navigating Dee's wheelchair over the speed bumps and down the steep level ramps, while navigating traffic in both directions. There were some eye-opening moments, but I managed to get her to the hospital reception in one piece and in a timely manner.

At reception, the staff could not locate the paperwork sent through by Dr P's office. You can only imagine the look Dee and I shared. It would take an hour and a couple of calls to Dr P's office to rectify the situation of the missing paperwork. To our surprise, Dee received an apology for the bungle that led to the delay. Now, that was a shock, an apology! Before progressing any further, Dee was required to place her John Hancock on a few dotted lines before escorted to the elevators and to the nurse's station of the floor, she would call home for the immediate future. For those who didn't understand the John Hancock reference, it is an American expression used to describe adding one's signature to a document, as John Hancock's signature appears prominently on the Declaration of Independence. Upon exiting the elevator, the nursing unit you don't always need to be interacting. Just being in the same room is enough.

Lunch was always a treat. She truly had no time for their offerings. As she often remarked, the best thing about lunch, the ice cream. How could I forget the day her ice cream failed to arrive! I was instructed to find its whereabouts. I'm being jovial. A nurse helped us out, returning with two ice creams in hand. I wondered why the two. I came to reason; since they overlooked her, the nurse took it upon herself to provide Dee with a double serve, sort of an apology. Boy, did I miss the mark! The second one was for me, and I was shocked; I was but a visitor. Dee pointed out that the nurse was flirting. Apparently, she had flirted on another occasion, and once again, I had no idea. I don't think she realised we were married, and I definitely didn't realise she was flirting. My wife had to point it out! Dee was okay with the flirting. She knew my love was unwavering and as she would often remind me; once she was gone, I needed to find love once more. Such talk made me feel uncomfortable.

While on the nurses, she would share the nurses' routine, with a wake-up call at the same time each morning and followed with a chat. I was the topic of conversation one day, the day I happened not to be in. They asked of my whereabouts, for I was one of the very few they'd seen with such dedication. They also discussed my quietness. Dee quickly corrected them, illustrating of my distaste for small talk and will avoid it when possible and further adding of my talkative nature, only when comfortable. I don't believe I truly spoke with anyone during her stay. My focus was on Dee.

Each evening, in preparation before leaving, I would tell how I loved her, kissed her, wished her a goodnight and come the morn; I would see her once more. It might not seem like much, but let me tell you, every word and every moment counts. Never take a single moment for granted.

Usually a few hours after my departure, Dr P would pop in every other night to talk about the cancer, answering any questions she may have and just shooting the breeze. Dee appreciated the humility and empathy displayed by Dr P. I couldn't begin to imagine his work load and yet, he would make the time to not only visit, but to interact on a person-to-person level.

Looking back, it is difficult to conceive how lonely she must have felt each evening. I was overcome with loneliness each night. How could I not feel lonely, for she was a part of me, a part of my life for more than half of my existence. Just reading that last sentence, it is mind boggling!

Reflecting upon the day of her scans, I had matters to address; unable to postpone. Although I wanted to be there, I knew she would be in and out all day and likely exhausted. I called before her first scan and she seemed upbeat and refreshed, having a well-rounded night's sleep, and complaining of her horrible breakfast. She steered the conversation onto the subject of finding love in the event of a poor outcome once again. Once she focused herself, there was no way you would or could shift that focus until she was ready. I never doubted she loved me and I know she was more concerned for me than herself. However, I didn't want to hear or take part in such a talk. Maybe it was my denial of the possibility of a poor outcome, or maybe it was my optimism. When you love unconditionally, you come together and make compromises and sometimes sacrifices when necessary. However, there is never any animosity.

We planned to speak again that night, giving time for her to eat and rest. However, she called early afternoon, catching me by surprise, but I took little notice. She may have been in-between scans, feeling lonely or wanting to provide an update. I had no reason to think any other way. That would all change when I heard the inflection in her voice. She didn't need to say a word; I knew. My heart sunk, my stomach was hollow, and my body numb. The x-rays revealed signs of the cancer having metastasised in the lower lobes of her lungs. As Dr P. mentioned, surgery might be an option, however, with decades of experience behind him, surgery was ill-advised. For what's seen, many more are lurking, invisible to current technology. We knew if the Chondrosarcoma spread (de-differentiated), the chance of survival…well, it wasn't what we wanted to hear. The realisation hit fucking hard. In a mere moment, hope erased. Dee would need a miracle!

Now, it was merely a matter of time.

She made sure that I had no plans for the Friday with Dr P. requesting my audience.

I cannot forget how fleeting that call was. Both of us trying to remain upbeat for the other, but the façade was crumbling, thus the briefness. Dad was with me and tact thrown out the window. I straight out told him; "the cancer's in her lungs, the remainder of the scans cancelled. This is it. She's dying!"

That night, I crawled into bed and just laid there in the cold, staring into the darkened abyss as the rain fell in my heart. The woman who meant the world to me was dying, and I couldn't do a damn thing to save her! My mind spent the darkened hours searching and reaching for radical notions…anything that may help, even thoughts of traversing space and time. You may laugh, but there isn't a thing I wouldn't have done to save her, even exchanging my life.

A sombre morning, accompanied with fatigue. The trip into the hospital, I was on autopilot. Walking down the corridor, the hospital was the quietest it had been. It was as if the news had spread. Usually, the television was on and the sound of our chatter would fill the room, but not today. We were still processing…the results…emotions…the reality. I stood gazing out the window, watching the bustling world continue. Periodically, a nurse would enter to let Dee know that Dr P. was still in a strategy meeting and would be around shortly. The brightness of the day transformed into a vibrant colour of hues before fading into the darkness of night. The day dragged out. I would come close to saying it felt as long as that Boxing Day all those years ago. With the night losing its youth, I was becoming agitated with the waiting. That's all we seemed to do, wait! Dee could see the agitation building and told me not to worry and to go home. Part of me wanted to, but I couldn't. Instead, I wandered the corridors to only bump into Dr P's assistant. He asked me not to leave; the doctor was making his way around. I would continue walking until I circled back to the room.

Dr P. arrived with his entourage in tow, totalling five. With the room filled, the door closed with a sound of authority, a solid clank. The energy in the room and just the visual pointed to less than optimistic news. Dr P. explained how the Chondrosarcoma had become de-differentiated. In this state, the cancer is an aggressive beast! The only way to determine and diagnosis de-differentiated Chondrosarcoma is to have the core biopsy sample extract from the mutated section of the mass. With no means of differentiating between mass and mutation, it comes down to blind luck. At the time (I assume it hasn't changed), there is no other method of determination. Once again, the importance of addressing the cancer quickly! In my opinion, the errors and delays lead Dee to this very moment. Dr P. continued to explain the x-ray findings and the limitations of current technology, furthering to describe the procedure conceived where the tumour surgically removed, along with healthy bone and tissue, allowing for clear healthy margins and a three-dimensional printed pelvis then implanted. Following the success, a course of radiation to remove any minute traces that may linger, followed by months or arduous rehabilitation.

For those who remember my remarks earlier about the ineffectiveness of chemotherapy and radiotherapy. That is true on the broader scale. For microscopic cells that may be present after surgery, it's proven that radiation to be successful.

I was standing on the opposite side of Dee's bed, near the window, when Dr P. asked if I had questions; also remarking how angry I appeared and was quite glad there was a bed between us. I explained how I had the utmost respect for everything done for Dee while under his care. What he accomplished in but a couple of weeks was more than anything accomplished in the months prior. I reserved my disgust and disdain for those involved prior to arriving at the office of Dr P.

Dr P. would utter two words that sent chills down my spine: 'life expectancy'. I looked across to Dee and she showed no reaction, taking it all in stride. On the optimistic side, her outlook was that of three months. The reality, based on experience and the aggressive nature of the cancer, her outlook was less than favourable, being that of a month; maybe.

Three months optimistically, but in reality, anything up to a month! How do you comprehend…where does one start? I wasn't about to give up on hope or a miracle.

Dr P. asked for the room as the entourage slowly dispersed, providing an opportunity for an honest and open conversation. Dee explained in great deal what she endured to just arrive at this point, to have a chance, even though the chance may be slim with all the errors. Dr P. was in disbelief, commenting that in his experience, if she had arrived sooner, there was likely a good chance that he could have operated. Dr P. didn't offer any guarantees, but from our research, she would have had a chance, a fighting chance. He explained how many discover their diagnosis by chance, with many a woman during childbirth. Dr P. would outline what to expect in the coming days, weeks and possibly months, recommending the use of a palliative care facility and even offered the current room and access to the team's care as long as she needed. Dee thanked him and politely turned down his offers. We agreed on palliative visits, but ultimately decided her last days would be at home. If she was to die, she would die at home, surrounded by love. We thanked Dr P. for everything, even though the outcome wasn't the one any of us wanted, although we expected it. You could see the disappointment in the eyes of Dr P. as he left.

No matter how you envisioned life, we are at the mercy of destiny.

I sat beside Dee, held her hand, just looking into her teary eyes. I pulled out my phone and played the first song that I played to her all those years ago through ICQ. It was a subtle hint of my feelings for her all those years ago and a reminder she still had my heart today. She knew me well enough to know what my other song of choice would be; John Lennon's My Life. It is a simple and yet powerful message of love.

I wanted to stay the night with her, but I just couldn't. Absorbing her emotions along with mine would have been all too much.

To this day, I cannot remember any part of the drive home, yet somehow I made it home without incident. Dumb luck, a touch of fortune, muscle memory or maybe a miracle?

We spent the next few days at the hospital arranging palliative care visits, pain medication, and her nutritional plan. The nutritional plan featured a couple of requirements, but she could basically eat what she wanted, when she wanted. If you thought the delays were over, you'd be seriously mistaken! Her return home, delayed because of the inability of two health districts being unable to communicate. On this occasion, it was our home district, in particular, palliative care holding up the process. Not a surprise and a sign of what we would expect later. Eventually, the issue resolved and Dee given the green light to head home. These delays denied her a chance of a fight, a chance of survival and now, a chance to spend time at home and time together. As I packed her belongings, those rostered on stopped in to wish her the best and to say their goodbyes. Dee was the type of person who meeting for the first time, you felt you had known for years. She just had that type of soul. It was lovely to see such a gesture. As I wheeled her out of her room, I was stopped at the door and direct left, as it was the quickest route to the elevators. Oh, how I would have loved to have known this piece of information earlier!

The challenge was ahead, navigating the unfriendly confines of the car park. At least, it would be easier working uphill. Yes, uphill. Downhill is a challenge, requiring considerable strength, for Dee could not assist if anything went awry. And although she was a shadow of her former self, it still doesn't make it any easier. Anyhow, on the trip home, we avoided any talk of the obvious and just spoke about anything and everything else. She mentioned she had a craving for a KFC wrap. Not the healthiest of choices, considering her nutritional plan, having cancer and just having left the hospital. What was the harm? It was a sign that she was feeling well, or at least better than she had. Usually, she was without an appetite. Would you believe there wasn't one KFC along our trip home? No matter, just a slight detour required. It shows I hadn't been to a fast-food establishment for some time, when you're surprised to see a dual carriageway drive-thru in operation. I looked across to Dee and we both burst into laughter. Seriously, one entry point, splitting into two, to then merge into a single lane. How could such a concept go wrong? With chaos and carnage avoided, Dee satisfied her craving and enjoyed the wrap. It was wonderful to see her enjoying food and I guess anything tastes better when compared with hospital food. Hell, I'll even throw in airline food!

The emergence of a new day and the beginning of a world filled with challenges and stress! Dee was determined to stay involved as long as she was able. I didn't want her to experience additional stress, but I understood where she was coming from. So, she took on the responsibility of the palliative care unit. As she would come to describe later, absolute fucking chaos! I was in charge of organising a bed and a few other things. All the while, I was thinking of the borrowed time, even more so now! We should have at least thirty or more years ahead to enjoy. How do you compress that length of time into but a few weeks or months? Dee was a fighter and I know when she heard her life expectancy, she was determined furthermore to prove everyone wrong, determined to celebrate our twentieth wedding anniversary. There was more than enough fuel driving her will.

Moving ahead, she conquered one short-term goal, the one month mark. That was a monumental positive, and yet, she continued to deteriorate before my eyes. Before me, the woman I love, even though she was but a shell of her former self. I fell in love with the person inside…her heart and soul. The rest was a bonus, also loved. Mentally, Dee was as sharp as always and a touch radical. She decided to experiment with a couple of natural remedies, one being empirical and the other somewhat experimental in the eyes of modern medicine, but seen as quite a useful herbal remedy in some parts of the world. As she looked at it, what did she have to lose? She was dying and maybe something positive could result from her death. The first, conceived to clear the lungs. Dee had begun to find it challenging to breathe, describing her lungs as feeling heavy. So, an equal weight of garlic to lemon was required for the recipe. Before weighing, the garlic peeled, the lemon remained whole, just washed. The lemon then cut into manageable pieces, the garlic added and blended down into a liquid. To reduce viscosity, water added. I couldn't imagine many enjoying such a beverage in a paste form. Next, the contents strained through a section of cheesecloth to remove unwanted lumps before being stored in an air-tight container and refrigerated. The air-tight container was not so much for freshness, as it was to suppress the pungent odour. Dee would consume a tablespoon three times daily, opting to go large and hard. The original concept was that of a teaspoon daily. Remember how I referenced the air-tight container earlier…you can trust me when I say there were no spirits lingering in or around the house once that seal broke. Still…more tolerable than chitterlings!

Our GP noted Dee's lungs before we started her experiment and checked during his visits. She remarked how she felt it had become easier to breathe and the heaviness she had described had since dissipated. The GP remarked of the change in the sound of her lungs. It didn't happen overnight; progressing over a couple of weeks and involving substantial bouts coughing. Although not scientifically proven or recognised, we believe it helped to clear her lungs. Do I feel there was an impact on the cancerous cells? I'm not a scientist and if I was to comment, I would say there may have been a level of impact, but not on a level of major significance. Nevertheless, that is but speculation. What I do know, it provided her with comfort, and that was important.

The second, I'd refer to as herbal remedy involving bitter lemon. One of Dee's work colleagues suggested bitter lemon. It is known for its nutrient properties and its wonderful source of power antioxidant compounds. There is also research that suggests it may have certain compounds with cancer-fighting properties. However, we were unaware at the time of the possible cancer-fighting claims. I would discover this some months before I penned this memoir. As with the garlic and lemon, the process was similar. The bitter lemon required to be sliced in half lengthways and the seeds scooped out, with the remaining flesh cut into cube sized pieces and blended.

Again, water added to reduce the viscosity. Dee would consume a shot glass between her garlic and lemon doses.

She would continue to lose her physical independence. There was nothing I or anyone else could do to slow or halt her deterioration. Her mind remained unaffected. She continued to enjoy filling in her Sudoku and in record time. Her handwriting revealed her unsteadiness. I attribute the unsteadiness to the pain and loss of muscle density. For most days, her appetite was okay to good. She ate her nutrient requirements and more. But for the amount she was consuming, she wasn't adding weight. The tumour...I would be confident in saying, equated to half of her body weight and likely more. It was immense! It had visibly grown and spread into her opposite hip and thigh and God only knows how much pressure and the displacement of her organs. Each time I needed to move her, I worried of the pain I may cause, as what muscle mass and fat remained, was nothing!

It was awful to see her in the state she was, but it didn't change the way I saw her and how I felt. I still saw the same woman I fell in love with all those years ago, and my love for her hadn't diminished.

Let's discuss palliative care and all that fun...I mean the bullshit.

To begin, there was one nurse who originally saw Dee and wouldn't see her again until the end, and she was great. We had no complaints, well...maybe one. The one complaint, she wasn't a regular sight, but that had more to do with the failing health system. Dee would be stuck with a nurse who was ill-prepared on most visits. She made her first appearance a day after the initial consultation, where all Dee's details were noted. That first visit, she arrived ill-prepared, having forgotten the paperwork at the office. The following week, she had the paperwork, but was unable to find the necessary information pertaining to Dee's medications and happened to be more interested in sitting and chatting. Maybe that was fine for other patients, but Dee didn't need or want someone to socially converse. She wanted a nurse who would actually check vitals, ask of concerns and/or issues and to examine her, considering she was bed-ridden and pressure wounds (more commonly known as bed sores) become a serious issue. Apparently, the nurse didn't share the same concern.

All of what I knew, I either learnt through my first-aid certification or the advice and lessons provided by Dee over the years. I am thankful for the knowledge and techniques. The one technique of moving an incapacitated person, I have come to use a few times, including with Dee.

Whenever palliative care arrived, I'd provide them with privacy. Although they had their privacy, I heard at times Dee's requests for certain things, more so pertaining to the treatment and care of pressure wounds. And yet, her requests seemingly fell on deaf ears mostly or postponed for further discussion the following week. The following week never seemed to arrive. Dee was forced to escalate her concerns.

During what would be her last visit from palliative care, the first nurse arrived and of course, in tow was Dee's favourite nurse! This would be the first time in weeks that she experienced a visual inspection. I did what I could to clean, maintain and prevent pressure wounds, but even for myself, I could not position her without assistance. No matter how creative or ingenious the notion, two people were needed. Inspecting her pressure wound, Dee's favourite nurse's inabilities had become a hindrance. I was asked to step in, positioning and holding Dee off the bed to allow unrestricted access. The procedure had taken quite some time and I reached a point where I needed to place Dee on her left side. Even if she wanted to help, Dee was too frail and in essence, I was holding dead weight. By placing her on her side, I could see the agony in her eyes, hear it in her breath, and feel the convulsions through her body. I felt awful; by holding her on her side, I was inflicting excruciating pain. I realise it was necessary, but it doesn't make it easier to accept. Never had I hurt her and just in this moment, I had inflicted so much pain.

How does any person willingly inflict pain on another?

After treatment of the pressure wound, the nurse remarked that the wound could have been much worse and acknowledged the treatment I managed had prevented a serious issue. Dee's pressure wound required two people, one to perform the required treatment and care, and the other to position and hold her. She restocked supplies (supplies that were requested weeks earlier) to maintain the wound and would return to monitor the situation. Treating the pressure wound not only took it out of Dee, but I also believe it shaved time from her fight. She had to withstand fifteen to twenty minutes of excruciating pain and stress that undoubtedly took a toll on her frail body.

Well, until that visit, it looked as if she was going to make our twentieth wedding anniversary. However, she hadn't given up the fight or fighting! I'd be lying if I didn't have negative thoughts creep into my mind. She was in pain, but on a level I couldn't imagine, and part of me hoped that pain would end soon. I just wanted her to realise it was okay; she had put up a fight that many thought unobtainable. It was okay to let go. No longer would she encounter errors and delays, no longer would she be in pain. I was proud of her. As she continued to fight, the selfish side of me wanted her to continue that fight. But my love for her knew it was only causing her pain.

The reality…no matter how determined she was, the beast was not only to win the battle, but the war. Our time together was now fading faster than before.

Everything would soon change, when my dad received a call from the hospital, the same hospital where Dee's troubles started. They knew of the families' situation; bringing forth his scheduled (minor) procedure. Like with any procedure, there are always risk factors and for Dad, his factors were uncommon if I was to judge by the odds. Dee had begun sleeping more frequently; a sign the end was creeping closer.

Dad would undergo his procedure a few days after the call. The procedure undertaken in the afternoon and by mid-evening, he was discharged, only to experience acute localised pain accompanied with a shortness of breath. He would return to the hospital via ambulance, where tests would reveal a punctured lung. Unbelievable! Seriously, what more can I say?

This would be a significant moment. Dad would now remain in hospital for the foreseeable future and it would mark the beginning of the end for Dee. On the day it all unfolded, she mustered up the strength to write a message, a message I would stumble across some weeks after her death. She couldn't take any more errors; she couldn't take what the health system had done to our family. First Mum, then she, and now the system could potentially claim a third life. She also asked God to look after and to protect me. Reading her message, I could see the absence of hope in her words and feel the anger and her love. Her message would contain some of her last thoughts. At a time where she knew her death was imminent, she still worried and focused on me.

Amazing…in her final moments of life, the health system would inflict a parting shot.

Sometime early Friday morning, Dee awoke finding it difficult to breathe. Helping to reposition her provided some relief. You cannot imagine the emotions I was fighting as I wrapped my arms around her and to feel her. The vivid memory of the day and I'm struggling to hold back the tears. We knew she would be lucky to survive another week. We needed to bring in help for her breathing. After a couple of calls, a portable oxygen unit arrived with a nurse in tow. The nurse would configure the nasal tubes and the unit. As the nurse was fitting said tubes, a glimpse of the old Dee appeared as she debated the best placement. It was a glimmer of light amongst the encroaching darkness. Before leaving, the nurse approached me and recommended that End of Life procedures begin. I already knew. The reality of the end was ever-so-real! Now, it was a matter of hours, days, or maybe weeks. Death was journeying, and her destiny was now within reach. They designated a P.E.A.C.H. pack; third-party nurses specialising in End of Life care, available twenty-four hours, seven days a week to assist myself and Dee. To hear those words, End of Life…my body fell numb. As the pack was unveiled, I was introduced to Marie, who would be the nurse in charge. She provided me with the rundown of the service, a tablet to communicate via video with staff, no matter the hour and what I should expect as death nears.

The uptake of oxygen was helping, as Dee's O^2 begun levelling out around ninety-seven percent, with spikes of ninety-eight and she was feeling much more comfortable breathing. Prior, her saturation had fallen, fluctuating between ninety and ninety-two percent.

That evening and into the morning, she slept more comfortably, but I could sense she was slipping away. I wasn't sleeping, just wanting to spend every moment I could with her. As I sat watching her sleep, my mind filled with many thoughts. Although she continued to drink plenty of fluids, her eating habits declined. Life is of signs, and the signs were all there. As she slept, I would speak to her with a soft voice, letting her know she needn't worry about me. I would be fine, for it was time for her to find peace and reunite with those she missed, reassuring her of her remarkable fight. She fought like no other I had known and she could be proud of surpassing Dr P's. realistic expectancy. I let her know it was okay to stop fighting. And here I thought making those phone calls when Mum died was tough. I was wrong. To ask her to relinquish the fight was brutal. Although heart-wrenching, I needed her to hear those words. She was far too focused on me. She needed to know I would be okay and now was the time she needed to focus on herself.

An aspect of love you never hear, reassuring the love of your life, even if you need to lie. This is a time in life when to lie is acceptable and forgivable, in my opinion. She would wake later that morning to eat some crushed ice. Coincidently, a P.E.A.C.H. nurse arrived for a scheduled check-in; provide anything she may need and help re-position Dee on the bed as to avoid further pressure sores. However, Dee had only awoken and still tired and made it clear she didn't want the nurse. She took no offence, explaining with her years of experience, even the kindest and gentlest of people can react adversely when in pain and in their final stage of life. She mentioned that Dee resting was more important at this point; along with her comfort. She would return tomorrow and if I needed anything, I was to either call or use the tablet. Only an hour after the nurse departed, Dee slipped into a coma, or what I believed at the time to be a coma. I hadn't experienced anything like this. My first call, to my GP. I described my observations, while providing O² levels, pulse and blood pressure readings. He suggested it was likely that she was in a coma and would be around at the earliest opportunity. My next call to P.E.A.C.H. and, by a stroke of fortune, Marie was in the area. On arrival, she examined Dee and confirmed my suspicion, highlighting Dee's time was now near. She explained how each of us is different, but from experience, Dee might have a couple of days at most, and to think of her focusing on familiar faces waiting to see her, and likely wasn't in pain. I felt my heart begin to break. For so long, I had held back the tears in-front of Dee. I was her pillar of strength, but I could no longer hold back the emotion; tears welled before flowing like a torrent. Marie consoled me; reassuring me that Dee knew I was there and could feel my love for her. Marie mentioned I needed to enact the final stage and made sure I was okay before leaving.

I called palliative care services and requested the final stage to the End of Life procedure be enacted. Requesting the End of Life procedure reminds me to this day, of sentencing her death.

Two nurses and my GP would arrive within minutes of each other, immediately jumping into action. Prescriptions written, the fulfilment of documentation and preparing everything else required. Organised chaos reigned! Before realising, I had a series of prescriptions in hand, prescriptions I was to fill, meaning I would need to leave Dee, and on a weekend evening, needing to locate a pharmacist open who may or may not stock the medication and the amounts. I found it to be absurd! The nurse informed me that under health policy, nurses were prohibited from signing out medications from the hospital, even small doses, to necessitate the ball rolling. Here I was on the phone chasing down pharmacies that were first open, who stocked the medications and had enough to fulfil the prescriptions. What a situation for the health system to drop a person in. There was no way that I was about to leave her side. No one in that room had any knowledge of the time she had left. There was no fucking way I was stepping a foot outside the house! I've always relied on myself and when Dee came into my life, we relied on each other. Reluctantly, I asked my sister for help.

Time was pressing and yet, it was non-existent.

Having sourced a supply, it would take my sister half an hour to three-quarters of an hour to return. The cost of the medications blew my mind. I knew there would be an expense, but such an expense! It didn't matter, she needed it and after all, it was but money. After some sorting, labelling and drawing, the nurse administered the first round of medications. I then underwent a crash course of how to draw, store, prepare the injection site and administer the various medications prescribed, manage the timing intervals and what to monitor and to identify. Once again, I returned to the mindset of five years earlier with Mum, having to disassociate. It's astonishing…in the space of ten minutes; I would be briefed and thrown into the proverbial deep end. The average person in a vulnerable and emotional state would not only find this challenging, it would likely be all too much!

That night, I didn't rest my eyes for a moment. Apart from monitoring and administering, I was squeezing every moment I could from the borrowed time we had left.

The following day, the situation remained unchanged. Was I expecting change...I think anyone in the same position would hope for a miracle! I made a call to a couple of long-time family friends who planned to visit the previous day, but due to unforeseen circumstances, couldn't make it. Undoubtedly, it was a tough call, letting them know of the situation, while offering the suggestion they need to visit today. My intuition was telling me it had to be today if they wanted the opportunity to say goodbye. Bryan and Margaret were family in essence, as you may remember from when I spoke of Mum's death. Family doesn't need to be of blood, at least not through my eyes. They were nearby throughout the entire turmoil. They visited as often as they could, at least once a week, even though they were no longer young of age and had their own health issues. I appreciated their visits and I know Dee did, even though towards the end, she would often fall asleep during their visits. Caring for her made it impossible for me to leave the house and her. They were aware and knew I was likely running low with food and other supplies as the garden crops; nearly depleted. Still, a few weeks of crops remained, mostly those Dee enjoyed. They took it upon themselves to buy an assortment of groceries. Although I felt awkward accepting it, I appreciated it more than they realise.

Bryan and Margaret arrived early afternoon and spent a few hours with her. I have to believe she was aware of their presence. Margaret was in tears throughout the entire visit, and Bryan, visibly shaken. I knew Margaret would struggle, as the two were close. As for Bryan, I had never seen him in such a state. As their time ended, Margaret hugged me, trying to contain her tears. I'll never forget what she said; "you two were meant to find each other. You complemented each other." It was now my turn to struggle to fight back the tears as I helped her into the car. Bryan and I shook hands and then hugged, as he expressed his sorrow and his disbelief. It was the first and only time that I had seen Bryan with tears welling in his eyes. As they drove off, my thoughts were with them. I only hoped the visit wouldn't place any undue stress on them.

It couldn't have been more than an hour give or take a few minutes, since they left. I spent that time sitting with Dee, reminiscing, describing the memories I had and how much I was in love with her. I continued to assure her, she needn't worry anymore and it was time for her to stop the fight…it was okay…it was time for reunions…with our child, her sister, Mum and many other people waiting to see her again. With her frail hand in mine and the clock chiming the seventh hour of the evening, she exhaled her last breath. The energy in the room changed…I felt her leave. Not only did half of my heart die, half of my soul died with her. Overcome with immense heartache and sorrow, I felt a glimmer of happiness. For now, she was no longer in pain. She was on her journey to magical reunions.

In-front of me, her body lay, just a hollow vessel and a reminder that a beautiful soul was now gone. No longer would I see her face or hear her voice; the woman I loved unconditionally…my best friend, my centre and my muse.

It was time to call my GP and the director of the funeral home. As I waited for their arrivals, I found it difficult to conceive she was gone and couldn't imagine a life where she wasn't a part of it. In an attempt to distract myself as I waited, I called to notify Dee's employer. As I mentioned earlier; what they did for her was truly remarkable. They didn't have to offer her any assistance, but they did, and we appreciated it. I then called Margaret and Bryan. God, this was to take everything I had. They had only arrived home a few minutes before taking the call. Bryan knew without needing to say a word. Honestly, I could not utter a word; I was not only choked up; I was in shock.

In the space of five years, I would lose two important women, and two women to the health system.

The first to arrive was that of my GP, solemn in appearance as he passed along his condolences. He would officially confirm Dee's death. Needing to prevent rigor mortis, I would assist him with a preventative procedure. Her body was an empty shell, and I knew she was gone. Nevertheless, I felt uneasy performing the task at hand, but he required assistance. Once satisfied, a preliminary death certificate generated for the funeral home. As he was preparing to leave, the funeral home arrived. A young woman and an older man arrived to receive Dee's body. As they went about their business, I couldn't help to think of the type of person it takes to work in such a profession. An empath would struggle to be immersed in such heartache, sadness, and pain. They treated her body with the utmost respect and dignity as they readied her for transport. The young woman asked if there was anything that she may have on her I would like them to remove as keepsakes, but all that was removed much earlier. To see her body placed inside that maroon body bag. The large silver teeth interlocking as the bag zipped, and to watch her body wheeled out; only finalised the reality.

How I wished this to be all just a sick and twisted nightmare.

Never did I feel as lonely as I did that night. The room, cold and empty and our bed, was not the same without her. I was numb…what was the use of waking if she wasn't there? She was my life…she was my everything. No matter how many times I tried to close my eyes to sleep, my heartache just wouldn't grant me such an escape. I lay there, staring into the darkness, the abyss of nothingness. My tears continued to fall like a deluge. Time slowly moving, if at all. The darkest part of the morning gave way to the dawns first light. Rays of golden light penetrated the darkened room, symbolising the birth of a new day and the first day without Dee. The first time in over two decades, she wasn't in my life. I dragged myself from the bed to stare in the mirror. There, a reflection of a man staring back, but I didn't recognise him.

That afternoon, I needed to complete the funeral plans, or should I say, lack thereof. Dee didn't want a funeral, like Mum. Both firmly believed that if you couldn't make the effort to see them while alive, then don't bother coming to cry and feel sorrow for yourself once I'm dead. It sounds harsh, but I do agree.

Before heading in, a detour was required. It was the first time since Dee's biopsy that I had stepped foot into the hospital. I spent some time with Dad, but my mind was at the furthest point of the universe, even though I know he was talking. I just didn't want to be there, in the hospital where this nightmare begun. I finally excused myself, making my way to the funeral home, where at the sit down, I was bombarded with question after question, from what type of coffin, how should she be dressed, will there be a viewing, a service or cremation, flowers, the number in attendance, her birth details, her occupation, details of her parents, their date and place of birth and death, occupation and so much more. Of course, I knew the information, but at the time and being less than twenty-four hours after her death, I was far from being in the right headspace. I confused some dates and outright forgot other details; all would end up creating headaches later down the track when I needed to amended her death certificate.

If you are wondering why the rush, it was Dee's wish, and I was not about to dishonour her.

In retrospect, I'm glad I was in shock, for when the invoice arrived, I would have unleashed a verbal tirade. To cremate a person with no service, just the basics…I cannot believe the cost! Dee didn't want to waste money on a funeral and other unnecessary costs. That money would be better served elsewhere. I will add, dying on a public holiday adds a significant amount! So, in the spirit of a public service announcement. If you're planning to die, make sure not to die on a public holiday, at least in Australia. Death is expensive; I knew that, but to conceive the figure in black ink on the invoice…unbelievable! I dread to imagine the cost if I had decided to go all out.

I was glad to be done with the funeral details and to be home. Scattered throughout, reminders of her. Of course, there'll always be reminders, but I still needed to deal with the bed, the O^2 unit and other matters. I didn't know where to start. Seeing as palliative care had arranged both, it seemed the logical point to begin. Not surprising, but my call, placed on a lengthy hold to only be informed I was required to return the O^2 unit from where I collected it. As I explained, the unit was delivered by means of a palliative care nurse. I did not collect the unit. Once more, I familiarised myself with the hold system. I was informed no record could be found indicating a unit delivered to my premises. I was then questioned if it was actually a palliative care nurse that I saw and received delivery of said unit. Fuck! I imagined it all; the nurse arriving, setting up the unit and the interaction between Dee and the nurse regarding the placement of the nasal tubes. Oh yeah…I was hallucinating the blue oxygen unit standing in the corner of my living room! "Serenity Now!" Back to the conversation and they advised me to locate a white or yellow sticker somewhere on the unit. That sticker would provide the details for support. Once I located the sticker, I was to call the number.

A wasted call and time I'll never get back! I already knew the outcome of the next call, but why not? Having punched in the number for the manufacturer's support, I began with apologising for wasting their time, before explaining the situation. They were quite astonished and I won't reveal the entire conversation. However, we enjoyed in a shared laugh! The next logical step; to call the liaison office of the hospital. Maybe I was going about this all wrong. Maybe I needed to think illogically! Having my call transferred through the switchboard, I explained the situation with the liaison office. From the liaison office, my call transferred to the 'appropriate' department, who could better assist me. I am sure you have a good idea where my call ended up! Oh, yeah! Right back at palliative care. Murphy! I can hear him laughing his arse off! Amazingly, I spoke with the same person for whom I spoke with less than an hour earlier. I recognised her voice, but I cannot say the same for her. I explained the situation once again, and she still failed to connect the dots. Whether incompetence or laziness, this had become an insane moment. However, insane escalated to a not-of-this-world moment when handed the same instructions! Well, if they didn't want their equipment returned, so be it! I had reached out, and it was out of my hands. When they realise the error of their ways, I'll gladly return it, of course, for a holding fee and an anguish fee!

I just wanted to be alone. The interaction with people was driving me crazy. However, forty-five minutes later, a nurse arrived to collect the syringe driver. I entertained the thought of asking her, but my logical mind thought better of it, for I knew she would point me in the hospital's direction. Once around, the merry-go-round was enough! However, I asked of how to dispose of the large quantities of medication I had remaining. Can anyone guess the response? Anyone? Her response; "I have no idea." What a system we have here! A grieving husband in the possession of medication, syringes and needles. All the essentials needed to take my life if I so chose.

I now see it. Rather than fixing the system, the idea is to reduce the demand on the system!

Having seen the back of the nurse, the first palliative care nurse who attended to Dee arrived. She had only been notified by the department of Dee's passing and took the time to check in. We chatted for a while. She was interested in how I was holding up and I spoke of Dee's last couple of days. As we chatted, the guy for the bed arrived and begun dismantling it.

I never mentioned the call regarding the bed, as it was a no hassles call, as you can determine. I threw caution to the wind, outlining the fiasco brewing. She couldn't understand why there was an issue, as the O^2 unit was the property of palliative care. She insisted I need not worry, as she would take it with her. Finally, a result that didn't have me in an infinite loop. I then chanced my luck with that small victory, asking of the medications and the procedure of disposal. As the words left my lips, I knew I was tempting fate and Murphy! She advised me to call the hospital and they should be able to direct my call to the appropriate person or department, capable of answering my question.

We all have our limits; some know their limits and others are yet to discover their threshold. I happen to know mine. A grieving widower or widow should not be placed in such a situation of unnecessary stress and left in the possession of substantial quantities of powerful medication. The system that's in place doesn't just need to change; it requires an urgent overhaul! However, another band-aid shall be slapped on to keep it all together, at least for another couple of months or years.

There was no way I was about to deal with the hospital again! It wasn't happening! I pondered the situation and called a local pharmacy I'd used in the past. The pharmacist was helpful, instructing me to collect all the medication, open and sealed packs, toss them into a large plastic bag and when convenient, just pop in, and they would dispose of it in the proper manner. It would cost nothing but time. At the pharmacy, I discussed of the difficulties; particularly finding assistance regarding the disposal of the medication.

You don't realise how broken the system is if you don't use it regularly. When you rely on the system, you come to realise there is a lot of luck involved.

For anyone who may encounter or knows of someone in such a situation; call your local pharmacy and ask them if they can dispose of the medication or if they can refer you to a pharmacy that can. The pharmacist should point you in the right direction.

I hope this bit of information helps.

The following weeks, I wasn't living...I was merely existing. The world I knew had forever changed; it had fallen apart, crumbling into the sea. I was lost without Dee. Over two decades; she had been an important and integral part of my life.

In the coming weeks, the grieving and heartache would amplify, having to close accounts, alter names on accounts, filing tax returns among a variety of tasks that couldn't be avoided.

Dee's tax return was essential, as it was tied to mine and pivotal for me to complete my return. It's amazing how fast information travels, having tried to access her online account prior to visiting the funeral home, to discover the taxation office had locked the account. Essentially forced to contact the taxation office. I must admit, the process wasn't difficult. I went into the call with the expectation of having to jump through hoops. They guided me through the process; a note pinned to my file, denoting no penalty in the event of a late return because of the death of a spouse. That helped to ease some stress. I was now required, as explained by the taxation office; to take either the original or a certified copy of Dee's death certificate and Last Will and Testament to a post office.

There it would be scanned into the system and the ball from that point would roll. Dee's Last Will and Testament caused problems with the Post Master, for it was not the original, although it was certified just like the death certificate accepted and scanned! I had the taxation's website open to the paragraph that stated either original or certified copy and pointed it out in the portal on the Post Master's monitor. Nevertheless, the Post Master refused to accept it and I would spend thirty-minutes pointing out the clear evidence to no avail. I could have continued, but he wasn't about to admit he was in the wrong. I returned home with paperwork in hand to return with the original. He rifled through the pages, as if he was looking for a reason to deny me once more. He found nothing and scanned the pages into the system. Next, I was required to supply identification, which I did, and that is where the next hurdle arose. The Post Master was now balking at my identification. His reasoning was that my names on my identification did not match the name used by Dee on her Last Will and Testament. However, three forms of identification provided three alternatives, one a direct match and the taxation office had all three variations in the system, whether middle name, no middle name or middle initial. After another debate and highlighting evidence on the portal, he conceded and scanned my identification into the system. Not to my surprise, but definitely his, the identification, authenticated and the process complete. A process that should have taken maybe ten minutes at most ended up taking more than an hour.

Now, all I needed to do was wait to receive the papers from the taxation office. Apparently, at the time, a final tax return could only be lodged and processed in paper form.

How I wish someone would have told me of the amount of paperwork I would face with the death of a spouse/partner. Some processes were free of hassle: fill out the form, provide identification, the Last Will and Testament and death certificate. Dee's superannuation was somewhat mixed. I was assigned a case manager, and the requirements were simple, and I wasn't expecting any delays or issues. From my experience assisting my dad when Mum died, the process was also relatively quick.

The weeks dragged, and I hadn't heard from my case manager. A call would be necessary to verify the status of my claim. He informed me the claim was currently in a hold status in relation to the cause of death listed. Well, Chondrosarcoma isn't a common cancer and few people have heard of it. When I mention it today, I am usually greeted with puzzled looks. He assured me the claim would be approved in the coming days.

With all paperwork completed, I turned my attention and time to turning two urns, one small and one large. I would turn the large urn from a pine tree topped a couple of years earlier and the smaller from an over-grown bottlebrush. It was a tough moment with the memories flooding back. The urns took longer than expected. It was a challenge to focus with the memories and that focus was imperative if I didn't wish to lose a digit or two. However, they turned out as I envisioned. I would receive the call to collect Dee's ashes having finished the urns. Once I had her ashes in hand, everything would be final.

The cemetery was a nightmare. My arrival coincided with a service. There was so much sorrow. As I sat waiting in the office, an array of random thoughts flowed until I glimpsed a few urns positioned on a display shelf. My jaw dropped when I read the price tags. One hell of a profit for all hands involved. Dee's ashes arrived in an unremarkable plastic vessel, accompanied with a paper carry bag. Before leaving, safeguards in-place enacted. I was required to verify the ashes in my possession were that of Dee. So codes and names needed to match to corresponding documentation. Having confirmed all was correct and in order, I left the office, making my way across the grounds and to the car park. Along the walk, I couldn't help to think of the last time I was here, being for Mum's service, a mere five years earlier. A service that went against her wishes. On that occasion, I was leaving with Dee beside me. And now, she is leaving with me, in my hands. Upon entering the car, although symbolic, this would be our last time travelling together.

Arriving home, I didn't waste time in preparing the urns.

To remove the plastic cap from the vessel according to the instructions provided was as simple as using a flat device, such as a flathead screwdriver, and working around the circumference whilst prying the cap. Let me say, it took some almighty work to remove that cap! It wasn't welded or sealed with any form of glue, just an extremely tight fit. I eventually removed it, destroying it in the process. There was no way that cap was going back on. So, if I had intended to remove but a small amount, well, I guess I wouldn't. So, a portion of the thousands of dollars spent went to the purchase and supply of a plastic vessel. For the money spent, one of the urns on the display shelf should have been provided!

Carefully, I transferred Dee's ashes across the two urns. With what little remained, I scattered across the garden beds. This was her home and she'll forever be a part of it, returning to become one with the earth. I tried my best to replicate her signature on the urn lid. A domed surface isn't the easiest to write on, let alone replicate another's signature and, of course, I'm no forger, as I have since discovered. Well, there goes my life's backup plan! It turned out okay. Being a perfectionist, I am my own worst critic. The smaller urn I turned specifically for my niece, I sealed the lid, for my niece and nephew enjoyed pushing the limits with each other and I could see an accident unfolding. For the larger urn, in essence, it was complete. However, I had ordered a small plaque, having yet to arrive.

I know Dee felt as if she was a burden in the end, but she wasn't. When you love unconditionally, you will do anything and everything possible; burdening is non-existent. When I took our vowels, they were a solemn promise from me to her. When I promise, I keep that promise. So, I'm reluctant to promise unless I know I can keep it. My love for her far exceeded the vowels and promise. Why I mention this, I am certain, some maybe wondering why I didn't admit her into a palliative care facility. It was my love for her, our love for each other and the desire to spend every moment we could with each other, and I wasn't about to chance anyone else looking after her. From the events that unfolded, I think I was justified.

Life is finite, and we just don't know when it is about to end. As we grow older, death becomes too frequent and our odds shorten. Life's perspective changes when death impacts directly. Life now is of living, loving, sharing and creating memories with that special someone; someone loved and cherished.

Dee's death rocked me to the core. Her death emphasised how important it is, to me at least, to share time with those who truly mean the world to me. Life is far more enjoyable, comfortable, and challenging when you have someone to love and share life. I know that some feel that I am a few sandwiches short of a picnic, and that is okay. We are entitled to express ourselves, and no person should be denied the ability to voice their opinion.

Time is far too precious, fragile and fleeting. Who wouldn't want to come home to the person they love, crawl into bed, cuddle them, laugh, talk of the future and share in the dreams…enjoying the moment!

True love doesn't find you at your best; it finds you when you're at your worst. That is important! Only a true love will see you at your worst and choose you…choosing and wanting to stay.

Chapter 12

The time had arrived to begin the next chapter and a new journey. Life is of chapters ending and that of chapters beginning, but where do you start as a widower? Widower, it seems so weird to say out loud and stranger that I am using it this early in life.

Dee knew I would be hesitant to begin a new chapter, or at least take the steps in the right direction, preferring a reclusive life and to hide my love away. It sounds quite appealing, never having to feel the heartache and pain of losing a lover and partner once more. But she knew me and, therefore, took matters into her own hands during the last couple of weeks of her life, and in secrecy. She somehow setup and created an online dating profile, something I was unaware of until I discovered a note she left with all the details. Was I impressed, no! She knew there was next to no chance that I would do it, let alone consider the idea of dating.

With the profile already established and curious, I explored this modern and strange world. I didn't know what to expect. Like with everything in life, things change and dating wasn't exempt. Browsing, I was far from impressed. Everything I absorbed just screamed 'commodity'. When did society sell its humanity? The madness behind the growing acceptance of a ghosting society was becoming clearer. What a society to live in! The expectation of connections to be instantaneous and the lack or want to keep relationships alive, rather spending energy and time finding fault. No longer do you need to confront the person, instead, the easy solution is to block and to jump back online, browse through the revenue-based algorithms and onto the next available person. I'm not about to apologise for expressing my opinion. I was quite happy to ignore it all, but I made a promise to Dee.

I took the time to read the profiles, finding many to be cut and paste like, all very similar. There were some who I found couldn't be bothered. If they couldn't be bothered; then what's the point? Why have a presence on the platform? A minority took the time to provide insightful information. With time, I would connect with two women; all provided unique insights into themselves that caught my attention, enough to pique my curiosity and left me wanting to discover more. It didn't take long to see that number halve, with one disappearing. And so, there was one! We chatted for a week or two, before moving away from the platform. In time, we took a chance, venturing into the pandemic dating world. Well, it was only the beginning of the pandemic and the chaos that would ensue. Honestly, I was shocked that she took a chance, and it was nice to get out and spend time with another person. From the first date, it was evident there was a lack of chemistry and that of a romantic connection.

It was an interesting time to date or to hang out. The city that once was alive with bustling crowds was but a ghost town, with the exception of a few rebellious souls and the giant rats! I'm sure some cats must have felt inferior and fearful. I remember the evening I glimpsed one and wondered when squirrels were introduced, and then I realised! To complete the ghost town scene, a spinifex blindly tumbling the desolate streets was required. Very few establishments continued to keep their doors open, and those who did, reduced their operational hours with fine dining only achievable by means of the isolation bubble. In other terms, a giant plastic bubble with a zip! Nevertheless, it was amazing to chat and explore the city with another; absent of the crowds. In other words, it was wonderful to be out in public, minus the public!

It was nice to remove myself from what had been my reality for some time. She knew of my situation, and it didn't bother her. It was a time where the world was changing and not for the better. Pockets of people were being isolated from friends and family, and that soon would expand outwards. We were two lonely people; different circumstances, but nonetheless, lonely who connected.

The COVID-19 pandemic had since gripped Europe and had grown; outstretching its influence. There was no pocket in this world now, safe from its influence. Restrictions and freedoms slowly eroded under the guise of health and safety. My continued journey would have my path intersect with Gee. I'm not sure what it was about her. There was something intriguing. She possessed inner beauty; for I am drawn to the inner beauty of a woman. I am thankful our lives intersected. We would end up chatting, eventually forming a friendship. For those curious, no, we never dated. The connection again wasn't romantic, nor do I believe it was meant to be, but situations and positions change. I just know our paths were intended to cross. We came to know each other. She possessed a valuable insight pertaining to a specific situation that involved my quest for answers and reforms of the health system. I am not ashamed to admit I was a fish out of water. I did not know what to expect or how to approach the situation and Gee was kind, warm and calming; guiding me through the process. Her insight was invaluable, and I owe her a great debt of gratitude. She need not offer her time or support, but she did. I was but a stranger to her.

Forever will I remember the days leading into that conference. Although reluctant, Gee insisted I read my statement. As she carefully listened, she provided incredible feedback and honed in on specific advice that helped me to refine my statement.

Gee may have the appearance of a tough and sassy exterior, one she outwardly displays. But I see through it. Curious by nature, I had to discover the mystery and unravel the intrigue. I am glad I did, for she is warm-hearted, empathetic, insightful, fiery, determined, compassionate and beautiful. Not only does she possess a beautiful soul, she carries a big heart.

Those few whom know me well, know of my selectiveness. I don't allow anyone into my life and rarely am I mistaken.

Her life is about to change for the better and I don't think she realises it or believes it. But who does until it happens.

Chapter 13

Life is a journey, for the better part, ingeniously conceived. When two souls collide, it is not by chance nor accident, it's by design. Sometimes, you're left wondering, well…at least I wonder, pondering the purpose.

This is where I'll introduce Lois. We met under unusual circumstances, but considering the times, unusual wasn't all that unusual. Those who lived through the pandemic will understand. Nevertheless, who in Australia could forget the brawls amongst supermarket aisles and the panic buying of toilet paper that created the Great Toilet Paper Shortage! Anyway, from the beginning, there was much I saw in Lois from her passion, strength, intellect, independence, compassion, sensuality, sexuality and vulnerability. If only I could foresee the future. If only. Unfortunately, life is a journey without cheat sheets or at least a manual! She intrigued me like no other had. I knew she would become someone important.

We shared in commonalities and mutual interests. Once again, there was a tiny issue…the pandemic! Lois had lived in Australia before the Great Toilet Paper Shortage, I mean pandemic, before returning home to her native country in the Americas to be with her family. At the time, we knew little of

COVID-19 and the pandemic that would soon unfold and reveal the true characters of many a person globally and give rise to the corporate elite. It didn't take Australia long, enforcing a COVID-zero mindset and policy, closing its international border, barring many, but not 'all' from entering and exiting the country, including its own people. A Federation of States would soon fracture as States and Territories were gifted power by the Prime Minister of the time. Excluding New South Wales, all other States and Territories would close their borders, denying families unity, people employment and vital medical services. Draconian measures instituted by a government and health system of the time made many feel imprisoned for a crime they did not commit. This would become a mammoth obstacle and a thorn in our sides. I have the opportunity to reflect, and I cannot help but to consider how today may have eventuated much differently. If our paths crossed some months earlier or the pandemic never developed; how different it may or may not have been? That is something we'll never know. Our paths were pre-ordained to collide at that moment, and I am thankful they did. Nevertheless, I still like to envision a different journey; I am only human, after all.

Talking with Lois came naturally; there was a sense of familiarity and comfort. Small talk was non-existent, no topic off-limits, and there was no subject we couldn't delve deeply into or share and enjoy a good laugh.

In the beginning, a time of discovery, a time of reminiscing of our lives and for her, reminiscing of her life and time in Australia. In the moment, Australia seemed a lifetime ago, but it was clear the country had captured her heart. Essentially, Australia was her home away from home.

I recall the story she shared of how she would come to arrive on these shores, or should I say, the influencing or serendipitous moment. She was in the right place at the exact moment she needed. Anyway, I'm glad it unfolded in the manner it did and she could enjoy the country that she would come to fall in love with. Australia and Lois are the perfect combination. For she is a child of nature; her soul revitalised with the caress of the saltwater and the sensation of the sun's warmth. Beneath her feet, the sands forever imprinted. I may be biased, but reality and the truth cannot be denied.

As our time progressed, it was undeniable how our comfort continued to grow, at least from my perspective. Conversations that started as messages would soon incorporate voice messages and further progressing into video calls thanks to WhatsApp. Come to think of it, we never had a standard voice call. Why waste time when you can just skip to the logical progression? Our video calls weren't all that regular to begin. Mind you, it was wonderful to see her and not just a photo.

Lois grabbed me like no other before.

Having mentioned her qualities earlier, as strange as it may sound, the video calls allowed me to feel her heart and to see her beautiful and seductive eyes. I cannot tell you how many times I forced myself to break eye contact because of her eyes! I must not and cannot forget her contagious smile. How could I not smile when she would smile? If I was having a rough day, just to see her smile would uplift the day. Her lurid voice, paired with zeal. I could sit and listen to her speak for hours on end. To my ears, her voice is soothing.

I remember the call in which I truly saw her eyes, focusing deeply into the windows of her soul. I'd been pondering the idea of a makeover; remembering how she mentioned I was hiding myself away. She was right. I don't think she realises how intuitive she actually is. Of course, I would decide to have the makeover during a pandemic! Why would I follow the rules of convention set by society? With extremely few businesses open, I took the plunge, although it took some time. Lois would be the first to see the change…the man no longer hiding, well, maybe from the world still, but not from her. It was during that surprise video call that I stirred a reaction in her. She noticed and pointed out that I was hiding, and she saw past the man hiding, to see into me. Her eyes were the widest I'd seen, her pupils dilated and her reaction…priceless! Eventually I would have the pleasure of seeing a similar reaction in the future, neither can be compared for each unique and treasured.

Why did I call to show her my new look? I think it is obvious. I was developing deeper feelings for her. I was oblivious to it at the time and now I realise it to be so. That seems to be a pattern with me, oblivious in such situations.

Only recently, at the time of finalising my first draft, did Lois share with me what was running through her mind when she saw my visual transformation. Listening to her describe her reaction was revealing. I only wish I knew much earlier. I would discover, no, realise, being the better wording, was how staring into her eyes would make my heart melt. I never uttered a word at the time, but knowing how she was beginning to know me more, I am sure she knew the effect she had on me.

I admit, I'm hopeless when it concerns the flirtatious advances of a woman. Hold on, the obvious I'm aware of, it's the subtleties. That part of my life I missed out. My childhood wasn't like the majority, dedicating myself in pursuit of my sporting dream. I had next to no female interaction, particularly girls of or near my age. From the age of twelve, most of my interactions involved adults, men and the few women, aged between their mid-twenties through to their sixties. Although I may have missed out on some aspects, I discovered much about life and the true world. Of course, with training and playing, there was little to no time to socialise if I desired. Anyway, I mention this as I am now sure there was many a time she must have been flirting, and I, oblivious! There is no other way to describe it. She must have thought I had no interest in her, as I wasn't reacting. Yeah, I noticed moments where she'd play with her hair; expose her neck and how she'd position herself. Of course, my pupils would dilate and I'm sure I had some goofy smile stretch across my face. If I did, she never let on and I think that was sweet of her. I would come to learn further about Lois' subtle indications with her guidance.

I would love to know her thoughts during this time. In the future, I hope to ask her and I'm sure we'll enjoy a laugh at my expense!

As we would speak of later, she believed I was still healing, but I wasn't afraid to disagree and I let it be known. I had come to terms with Dee's death, and of course she will always hold a piece of my heart, but this heart of mine has room to love another, like Lois. I may have been apprehensive, as I was unsure how to move forward. But her soul shone bright; a guiding light.

Of course, she was interested in discovering more about Dee and I was happy she was interested and I think it's not only important, but healthy. Certain aspects I didn't feel comfortable in sharing, particularly a video call; I wasn't sure how she may react to the emotion. I promised to share with her when we meet and I'm a man who keeps his promises. For those wondering of the emotion, I don't intend to withhold details and some details are heart-wrenching.

As Lois opened up of her past relationships, I was torn. There was a part of me that became guarded, for some people never truly overcome such events. On the other hand, I couldn't but feel for her and I only hoped she was ready and, honestly, I was hoping she would accept me. How and why such a beautiful woman inside and out needed to experience such moments, leaves me absent of reason! I just find it difficult to understand the actions of some people. We can learn much if we opened our eyes and observe the animal kingdom. I reassured her that the past was just that, the past and it has no control over her or does it define the woman she is today. We learn from the moments and move forward, for the future is ours to make.

Maybe I possess a utopian or merely an askew view regarding love and relationships. Maybe I'm evidence that either parallel universes exist or time travel is possible.

I see so many lusting and believing it to be love, only to have their worlds come crashing down around them. It's important to build a friendship, for that person will not only be your partner and your lover, they will be your best friend. Friendship is the core to establishing a solid foundation, for all relationships need a solid foundation to build. Could you imagine building a house upon a shoddy foundation!

With the months endlessly continuing to roll, our familiarity grew on multiple levels; discovering such preferences and favourites as colours, scents, music, foods and an array of other likes, loves and dislikes. It was around this time my feelings had shifted positively. Indeed, we hadn't met in the physical, but for the moment, our hands remained shackled. We had plans of meeting. It was frustrating knowing there was this unique and beautiful woman who I shared an amazing connection and we were at arm's length. There was a point where I seriously considered building a boat to sail the Pacific to her. I am serious! I couldn't fly nor could I jump on a cruise ship. I even made fun of the idea in passing during a call. She enjoyed a laugh, but not for the reason I was laughing. She would come to tell of a South African man who sailed his way to the Americas during the pandemic. Nevertheless, the universe had our paths intersect and our souls collide. Let's not forget, the heart chooses who it desires. Who am I to intervene and disrupt a process that is far greater than you or I!

What I would have given to teleport to her! We have mobile phones, smart watches, virtual reality headsets; big screen televisions. When you think about it, each concept featuring on Star Trek at one point, and yet, what happened to teleportation?

As we have established, typical me. I refrained from pursuing my emotions at the time. With an end to the lockdowns nowhere on the horizon, I thought it wiser to allow my emotions the freedom needed, whether my feelings would continue to grow for her, or if they would slowly fade.

The days and months continued to drag, much having to do with the damn pandemic and lockdowns! Lois had slightly more freedom than I as the pandemic was now becoming not only a hindrance, but an annoyance. The source of the drag seemed to be the minority, those capitalising on the misery of billions. My feelings for her had only intensified. However, I still was hesitant! Not of myself, but of her feelings. Was she flirtatious to pass the time, or did she have genuine feelings? After all, we are but fallible humans. We do all we can to avoid rejection, for rejection is the bringer of pain. Still, I held on to this little secret for a few more weeks to come. Leading up to and during this period, our video calls became more frequent and the use of emojis more prevalent in our messages. Probably the most noticeable difference was how we became active in each other's everyday lives. What I was sensing was of the connection moving past the general friendship level and becoming more intimate. I know, how could I sense the connection becoming more intimate and unable to identify a flirtatious advance! That is a rabbit hole I don't think any of us want to travel down.

Whether friendship, dating or a relationship, distance shouldn't play a factor, especially in dating and relationships, for distance should only be temporary. Indeed, distance makes intimacy a challenge, but it shouldn't alter the emotion. When I refer to distance being that of temporary, you should make plans, whether to connect for the first time, to share quality time by way of a holiday or to make a more permanent decision.

While distance keeps you separated, both parties have to be committed and able to communicate, for communication is of the utmost importance! Anything of significant importance cannot be set aside for a later date, where it may fester; it needs to be addressed in the now and via a video call. Texting is just the perfect way to miscommunicate and misinterpret words, phrases, context, infliction and emotions. When communication falters, it not only becomes an uphill challenge, but a testing fight. And, if you are a lover, then you are a fighter and you'll fight for love. But, not everyone is a fighter and not every challenge has a successful outcome.

As I have learnt, life is not as it appears. Life has a habit of keeping you on your toes.

I hope Lois realises how uniquely amazing and beautiful she is. I also hope she'll open her heart and allow me to love and take care of her heart, as she deserves to feel that of unconditional love.

A slight detour, but necessary; nonetheless. Life can and often changes in the blink of an eye. She deserves to experience the emotion and sensation of being loved unconditionally and that of selflessly by a partner who is by her side during the tough times, who will celebrate with her during the best of times, and someone who will support, care, and champion her. Someone who is excited to see her and the relationship grow.

Back on track, and my feelings hadn't diminished, and I'd be lying if I didn't hope the person she would chose and want, would be me.

Chapter 14

I started writing this memoir or maybe I should call it a true life love story, late 2020. The pandemic continued as the lead of every news cycle. There was no escaping it or the apocalyptic messaging from health officials and political leaders. As I sit in-front of the keyboard typing, 2022 is rapidly coming to a close and a fresh New Year is lurking on the horizon; a year pending certification.

There was a point where I thought I'd be happy ending with the previous chapter, but the more the idea meandered amongst my thoughts, I realised, not only wouldn't it be fair to myself, it didn't seem appropriate. The situation with Lois was continuing to unfold, and we needed time to see what may or may not eventuate.

Lois is well aware of her inclusion and her importance. Albeit, not her true identity. Actually, she was the first person I shared the news of a recent achievement and success.

I can imagine many of you are wondering when I'm about to spill the proverbial beans. I can feel the tension and the want. Well, you'll just have to be patient, for I will need to write the sequel. Just kidding! I have no wants of a sequel, but a sequel could be warranted and quite interesting.

The connection we share, I would say, is unique. Not surprising, for she is unique. Lois is not only special, but she is important and I know she shares that feeling. That I can say, for we have spoken of this only recently. Well, by the time you may very well be reading this, you might want to omit recently! For me, there was a moment very early in our developing friendship where she shared a photo of her and her family on holiday. Quite an intimate moment, considering we really knew little of each other, and she chose to share it. That not only validating what I saw and felt in her from the very beginning, it further emphasised her heart and soul. I knew I found someone who I felt comfortable with and could call a friend. Someone who would see all that is hidden to the rest of the world.

Although closing a dreadful chapter of my life and beginning anew, I would choose to open this new chapter with the following: "For history shall repeat for the ignorance and greed of humankind knows not of its limitations…" That opening describes what awaited humanity; the COVID-19 pandemic. During this not only challenging, but difficult time, we shared many a moment and a few choice words. Her words filled with distinct passion. What I will share is how she is one of few; past and present who has the ability to have me talk about myself without redirection. I have no idea how she does it!

Although a terrible period, it rates as one of the memorable periods of my life.

Of course, during this period, there were other memorable moments. The earliest moment was her birthday; it was her first birthday since we met. She had the opportunity to celebrate with her family. I wished her a happy birthday the day before, for that reason. It was her day to celebrate with her family, especially with an opportunity to do so during the pandemic, and I had no intention of disturbing her. However, she wanted a video call and asked if I would call; I politely declined. I knew the celebrations and the day would be long and she would likely be tired and wanting to spend time to herself and rest. Apparently, my declining was far from the answer she wanted to hear. Let's just say she was persuasive, and I would make that video call for her birthday! I soon discovered her determination and her persuasiveness! That was but one moment. There were other moments of happiness, laughter, frustration, sadness, and tears. The moment she had me, maybe I should say won me is one I'll never forget, but that is for later.

I found myself fortunate and honoured to see her re-build her career…her passion. To see where she was and where she is today, she has come such a long way, conquering so much, and I am so proud of her! She deserves to enjoy the success and every moment to come, for there is more success to unfold. You'll just need to trust me.

Whenever she spoke of her career, it was always with enthusiasm and passion. Her career was not only important to her, but to those who sought her knowledge and help. As I've told her, I am her biggest silent supporter. I have suggested her expertise to people who now read her many posts, finding them insightful, knowledgeable and helpful.

Never would I interfere or stand in the way of her career. Lois and her work are far too important and I have much respect for both.

I guess it's time to reveal the moment Lois had me or won me. We were engaged in conversation and out of the blue; she spoke of a piece of text from a book she read that reminded her of me. The text was penned in Portuguese. She shared the piece, and not only did it touch my soul, it touched my heart.

By the time she sent it to me, I knew I was in love with her and it revealed what she had yet to say. However, the text, the context and her action spoke louder than words could. The quote loosely translates into "You touched me without having to touch me." I say loosely, as with all translations, words can become lost in translation or there is simply no translation for the word. Intense emotions, captured within beautifully written text.

We drifted apart for a bit of a spell, only to find our way back to each other. During that time apart, we remained in-touch. Each; important to the other. How could we not remain in-touch? Some may find that difficult to believe. In that time, I would come to see the unseen. Nevertheless, during that time, never did I stop loving her. How could I stop loving the woman who won my heart? In my eyes, she is the most beautiful woman on this giant rock hurtling through the galaxy. Also, allow me to clarify, when I use the word 'beautiful', I am referring to the beauty I see not only externally, but the beauty within.

As of today, our love for one another hasn't diminished…I feel it has grown.

I can hear many of your thoughts…you haven't met in the real world…in the physical! That is valid. However, I can say, I have since returned from the UK where Lois and I spent time together, time that confirmed what we had felt for each other. Unfortunately, our schedules weren't perfect, and she was a little hesitant. so the trip was a quick one and now, the missing begins. There were memorable moments during the trip, two happening on the same day. The first day we caught up, was far from spectacular. The gloomy morning; cold, wet and blustery. As I made my way to our meeting point, having a little too much faith in maps and the lack of street signs, I was forced to take a moment to gather my bearings. Lois serendipitously walked by. (Normally, I don't respond to my name called in public.) She spotted me immediately, calling out my name. Without hesitation, I recognised her voice. We shared an awkward hug. It's not easy to hug with umbrellas in blustery conditions. Why I refer to it as serendipitous, is that she hadn't my SIM number for the UK, so without Wi-Fi, there was no way to reach me. If our paths didn't cross at that moment, we likely would have missed each other that day. Lois for only knowing me through video calls and photos was able to pick me out when I had the umbrella covering my face.

If you remember how I spoke of her reaction to my makeover and I mentioned there being another moment. This is that moment. We found a cosy café, each enjoying a hot chocolate as we chatted, catching up with each other and life in general. Her birthday was but a couple of weeks earlier and I had hoped to be there at that time, but it wasn't meant to be. Even so, I hadn't nor would I forget her birthday. With me, her birthday gift. I know she didn't see it coming! Lois is not the easiest person to surprise…she is a super sleuth! Anyhow, I mentioned I had a gift and of her birthday and handed her a small blue box. Let me say, the look on her face and her body's reaction when she opened that blue box and feeling her energy was priceless! It is another moment forever ingrained into my memories.

Our physical meeting was a surreal moment. I'm sure we were both excited and apprehensive that after two and half long years, the moment we had dreamt of, was no longer a dream, but that of reality. Because of that, I know I didn't truly consider the what if's! What if our feelings were true? What if the chemistry was undeniable? I wish I had at least stayed a week or two longer. The purpose behind the trip was to physically meet and to gauge our emotions, chemistry and other factors. Caution played a small role in my decision making, as did her schedule and me not wanting to overstay or to give the feeling I was pressuring. Accommodation costing and availability played a major role. Geez! When a decent hotel was considerably cheaper than an Airbnb…that speaks volumes of the effect the lockdowns had on people.

I never thought the missing would impact me as much as it has. I do miss her every day. Now, we have video calls and messages, but there in the UK, we could organise something for the next day or later in the week and spend that time together. She has an amazing soulful and physical presence.

The moment I stepped on that plane homeward-bound, I left my heart with the woman I left behind.

That trip across was long, but also filled with excitement! The trip home, agonisingly longer! During my stop-over, I recorded a video for Lois. It was difficult. It took me at least twenty attempts to produce something presentable. I undoubtedly knew she would have an impact, but I never conceived such an impact. Maybe it's because I am getting older and maybe it has to do with Lois and my deep feelings for her.

Nevertheless, we're actively communicating and in the process of working out the when and where we'll next spend time together, having narrowed it, with a preferred destination. Unfortunately, since the pandemic, very few things have returned to the same level or close to the level, pre-pandemic.

The universe propelled us together, and the universe is truly making us work for this connection! Life wasn't meant to be easy, nor was it meant to be this challenging. Those challenging connections provide the greatest and most satisfying rewards.

Although brief, the time I spent with her was magical! She is the person I had come to know. Her presence…I'm trying to find the words…at the moment; all I can conjure is wow! I'm left speechless. To finally gaze into her eyes, to see the beauty there within; my heart melts every time. To hear her speak, always fuelled with passion; as I mentioned earlier, I could listen to her all day. Her voice is soothing and sultry in the same tone. She may not realise, maybe she will if she reads this, and seeing as I have shared these chapters with her, I'm sure she knows. She has taught me much, not just of herself and nutrition, but life. And, I still have much to learn.

Of course, how can I forget her smile! As I mention previously, I cannot help but to smile when I see her smiling. She achieves something that very few have managed; bring a smile to my face. When I talk of a few; you can count the number on one hand with ample digits to spare.

I realise our temporary absence has only been a few weeks at the time of writing, and yet it has been difficult for me. Lois fanned and fuelled the smouldering ember within me. I thought I couldn't and would never love again, and she appeared. She is the inspiration behind many of my words, whether poetry, inspirational messages, or many of my other writings. In one form or another, she is never far from my thoughts.

I remember with vivid sensation and emotion the moment I first held her delicate hands; the first time we held each other, hearing her breath change and I still have moments, where I can smell her in waves. And how could I forget our first kiss, to kiss and taste her sweet subtle lips. Even my vivid imagination never came close to that of the moment! It's difficult to remind oneself that the missing is only temporary.

At least, Lois saw the two sides to me, the quiet and mysterious public figure and the private me; the affectionate, the humorous, the passionate and the thinker. She is one of three people to have seen me and after all, she did see past the man hidden all those years ago. I think she may have been a tad doubtful or didn't understand what I meant when and how I referred to myself over the years in our calls until now and that is understandable.

I desire to hold and kiss her again. The romantic in me hopes it will be forevermore. Nevertheless, it does take two to samba and I guess time will reveal all. Having said that, one needs to trust their intuition. For it is our greatest asset, for it sees the nuances and secrets; revealing all.

Although this is but a tiny snippet of my journey, I've come to discover and learn how fragile and fleeting life truly is. We take for granted that we have x amount of years ahead of us, when in reality, we just don't know when it will all end. Of course, no wants to think of death, let alone their loved one's mortality. For all that I know, these could be my final hours along my journey. I just don't know! If it should happen to be, I can say with confidence that I have lived my life and that I have cherished the moments and memories. The only disappointment would be that of not spending more time with Lois. Nevertheless, every moment resides within my memories and heart.

I might not know why I am here, but I can say I'm where I need to be, even though I wonder if I was made for these times. Then I reflect on the moments and lives I've impacted and my intuition tells me, all that has unfolded has led me to this very moment.

Final Thoughts

I will thank those who managed to make it to this point. I either kept you captivated throughout or the suspense was too much to bear and you just had to know how it all ends. Well, it has yet to end and I am hopeful there is more to come.

I would like to take this opportunity to share some thoughts with you.

Often we can find ourselves looking to others for the answers we seek. The answers you seek reside within you. Sometimes we need a non-judgmental ear we can trust, for speaking outwardly can break down the barriers that prevent us from unearthing the answers.

Contrary to the beliefs of many, a relationship doesn't kill your independence, nor does it interfere with your pursuits and goals. Indeed, you'll come to rely on each other along the journey, but only you can allow your independence to diminish and vanish.

And on a final note, remember to grow together and not apart. Communication is not just important, it is crucial. Be clear with your needs, your wants, your desires and your boundaries and be courageous! And when you may feel the other isn't listening, usually it's because something was lost in communication, so take the time to talk it over once more.

In a relationship, you love each other, you support each other, you want the best for each other and you want to see each other succeed. Remember to engage in those uncomfortable and sometimes difficult conversations and never forget to make time for each other; that of emotional and physical intimacy. Neglect will serve nothing more than to lead you down an unnecessarily challenging path. And most importantly, if you're an unconditional lover, you are a fighter.

Life is ultimately better when you have someone you love to share in the experiences and the memories; someone to create those forever moments. That someone you can come home to, who'll want to hear of your day, who'll care for you, who wants to cuddle and forget the worries of the day.

Remember to live, be not afraid to love with all your heart!

Made in the USA
Monee, IL
03 May 2026